SUPER-FAST
Slow
Cooking

Toss it in, turn it on...quick-prep recipes with only **5 ingredients**. What could be easier?

Gooseberry Patch
2500 Farmers Dr., #110
Columbus, OH 43235

www.gooseberrypatch.com

1·800·854·6673

Copyright 2008, Gooseberry Patch 978-1-933494-55-5
Seventh Printing, September, 2010

Do you have a tried & true recipe...

tip, craft or memory that you'd like to see featured in a **Gooseberry
Patch** cookbook? Visit our website at **www.gooseberrypatch.com**,
register and follow the easy steps to submit your favorite family recipe.
Or send them to us at:

Gooseberry Patch
Attn: Cookbook Dept.
2500 Farmers Dr., #110
Columbus, OH 43235

Don't forget to include the number of servings your recipe makes,
plus your name, address, phone number and email address.
If we select your recipe, your name will appear right along with
it...and you'll receive a **FREE** copy of the book!

Contents

Dedication

Dedicated to families
everywhere who love
home-cooked meals
without the fuss!

Appreciation

For opening your recipe boxes
and sending us your best,
a heartfelt thanks!

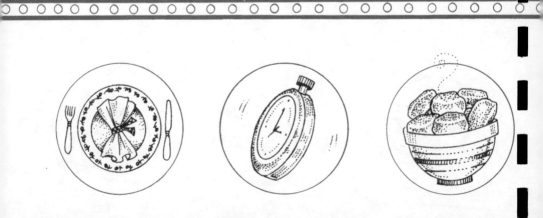

Chicken & Turkey

Down-Home Chicken & Noodles

Alicia Palmer
Greenville, OH

My family loves this dish...it tastes like you've been cooking all day!

1 lb. boneless, skinless chicken
    breasts
salt and pepper to taste
2 10-3/4 oz. cans cream of
    chicken soup

14-1/2 oz. can chicken broth
16-oz. pkg. wide egg noodles,
    cooked

Place chicken in a slow cooker; sprinkle with salt and pepper. Top
with both cans of soup. Cover and cook on low setting for 6 hours,
or until chicken falls apart. Remove chicken from slow cooker and
shred. Return chicken to slow cooker; add broth and cooked noodles.
Mix well. Cover and cook on low setting for an additional 30 minutes,
or until heated through. Serves 6.

Resist the urge to lift the lid of your slow cooker
to take a peek! Lifting the lid lets out the heat and
makes cooking time longer.

Southern Chicken & Dumplings

Stephanie Lucius
Powder Springs, GA

A great-tasting homemade dish...with almost no effort!

3 10-3/4 oz. cans cream of
    chicken soup
1/4 c. onion, diced
6 boneless, skinless chicken
    breasts

3-3/4 c. water
3 12-oz. tubes refrigerated
    biscuits, quartered

Pour soup into slow cooker; add onion and chicken. Pour in enough water to cover chicken. Cover and cook on low setting for 6 to 8 hours, or on high setting for 4 to 6 hours. About 35 to 40 minutes before serving, turn slow cooker to high setting. Drop biscuit quarters into slow cooker; stir well. Replace lid and cook for 35 minutes more, or until dumplings are done. Stir and serve. Serves 6.

Slow cookers are ideal for any country supper potluck.
Tote them filled with your favorite spiced cider, stew,
pulled pork or cobbler...scrumptious!

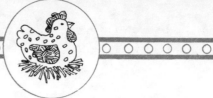

Joan's Chicken Stuffing Casserole

Joan Brochu
Hardwick, VT

Hearty and so filling, this chicken dish will be the first to disappear at any potluck.

12-oz. pkg. chicken stuffing mix
3 10-3/4 oz. cans cream of
　chicken soup, divided
3 to 4 c. cooked chicken, cubed
1/2 c. milk
12-oz. pkg. shredded Cheddar
　cheese

Prepare stuffing mix according to package directions; place in a slow cooker. Stir in 2 cans of soup. In a medium bowl, stir together chicken, remaining soup and milk. Add to slow cooker. Spread shredded cheese over top. Cover and cook on low setting for 4 to 6 hours, or on high setting for 2 to 3 hours. Serves 6.

Toss together a side salad in a snap. Combine finely chopped lettuce with chopped romaine, Genoa salami, mozzarella cheese and canned garbanzo beans. Simple, but oh-so good!

No-Fuss Turkey Breast

Pat Wissler
Harrisburg, PA

With only 3 ingredients, prep time is amazingly fast.

5-lb. turkey breast
1.35-oz. pkg. dry onion
   soup mix

16-oz. can whole-berry
   cranberry sauce

Place turkey breast in a slow cooker. Combine soup mix and cranberry sauce; spread over turkey. Cover and cook on low setting for 6 to 8 hours. Makes 6 servings.

Mom's Turkey Breast Dinner

Penny Sherman
Cumming, GA

With potatoes and carrots, this is a complete meal in the slow cooker.
I simply round out dinner with a side salad and cranberry sauce.

4 potatoes, peeled and sliced
4 carrots, peeled and sliced
2 to 3 lbs. turkey tenderloins

10-1/2 oz. can French onion
   soup

Place vegetables in a slow cooker; add turkey breast. Pour soup over top. Cover and cook on low setting for 6 to 8 hours. Serves 6.

Spray the panels of a door with chalkboard paint and let dry...a clever chalkboard the whole family will love! It's just right for sharing what's on the menu tonight.

Homestyle Turkey with Stuffing

Nancy Wise
Little Rock, AR

There's just nothing like the aroma of turkey and stuffing!

1 T. olive oil
1 onion, chopped
2 T. apple jelly
6-oz. pkg. turkey-flavored
   stuffing mix

3/4 c. hot water
2-lb. boneless, skinless turkey
   breast
salt and pepper to taste

Heat oil in a skillet over medium heat. Add onion and cook for 5 minutes until golden, stirring frequently. Add jelly and heat for one minute longer. Spray a slow cooker with non-stick vegetable spray. Place stuffing mix in slow cooker; drizzle with water and mix gently. Sprinkle turkey with salt and pepper; place on stuffing mix. Spoon onion mixture over turkey and spread evenly. Cover and cook on low setting for 5 to 6 hours. Makes 5 servings.

When they're available, fresh herbs really add flavor that's so much better than dried or ground herbs. Picking them straight from the herb garden makes a flavorful addition to summertime slow-cooker meals!

Bacon-Swiss BBQ Chicken

Michelle Crabtree
Lee's Summit, MO

This is a great recipe requested time and again in my family.

6 boneless, skinless chicken
   breasts
26-oz. bottle barbecue sauce

6 slices bacon, halved and
   crisply cooked
6 slices Swiss cheese

Place chicken in a slow cooker; cover with barbecue sauce. Cover and cook on low setting for 8 to 9 hours. Arrange 2 strips halved bacon over each piece of chicken; top with cheese slices. Cover and cook on high setting until cheese melts, about 15 minutes. Makes 6 servings.

Serve up a tasty slow-cooker meal and host a toe-tapping, Texas-style cookout! Just for fun, wrap dinner rolls in bandannas to keep warm, then tuck them into a bread basket.

Garlicky Bacon Chicken

Lisa Robason
Corpus Christi, TX

Easy and elegant...makes a divine creamy sauce to serve on top of wild rice.

8 slices bacon
8 boneless, skinless chicken
  breasts
2 10-3/4 oz. cans cream of
  mushroom with roasted
  garlic soup

1 c. sour cream
1/2 c. all-purpose flour

Wrap one slice of bacon around each chicken breast and place in a slow cooker. In a medium bowl, whisk together soups, sour cream and flour. Pour over chicken. Cover and cook on low setting for 6 to 8 hours. Serves 8.

Baked potatoes are yummy with any dish, and with a slow cooker, so easy to prepare. Simply use a fork to pierce 10 to 12 baking potatoes and wrap each in aluminum foil. Arrange them in a slow cooker, cover and cook on high setting for 2-1/2 to 4 hours, or until tender.

Aunt Jo's BBQ

Marilyn Godfrey
Stephenville, TX

I first made this when I was 16...and I still think it's good at 61!

4 lbs. chicken	2 t. pepper
4 t. mustard	1 c. vinegar
4 t. chili powder	

Place chicken in a slow cooker. Combine remaining ingredients; pour over chicken. Cover and cook on low setting for 6 to 8 hours, or on high setting for 3 to 4 hours. Makes 6 servings.

Sloppy Joe Chicken

Kathi Downey
Lompoc, CA

This is super for any game-day meal...it cooks up while you're waiting for the next touchdown!

6 chicken thighs	8-oz. can tomato sauce
1-1/2 oz. pkg. Sloppy Joe mix	cooked rice
2 T. honey	

Place chicken in a slow cooker. Combine remaining ingredients except rice; pour over chicken. Cover and cook on low setting for 6 hours. Serve over rice. Serves 4.

To get a slow cooker to work its best, always fill it from 1/2 to 2/3 full of recipe ingredients.

Chicken with Mushroom Gravy

Jo White
Philadelphia, TN

It's easy to double this recipe...just use a larger 5-quart slow cooker.

3 boneless, skinless chicken
    breasts, halved
salt and pepper to taste
1/4 c. chicken broth

10-3/4 oz. can cream of chicken
    soup
4-oz. can sliced mushrooms,
    drained

Place chicken in a slow cooker; sprinkle with salt and pepper. Mix together broth and soup; pour over chicken. Stir in mushrooms. Cover and cook on low setting for 7 to 9 hours, or on high setting for 3 to 4 hours. Serves 4.

To make a bigger batch of a favorite slow-cooker meal, remember these handy tips for doubling or tripling the ingredients:
- Always brown beef or pork to help it cook more evenly.
- Go ahead and double or triple the amount of meat or poultry, but only increase the seasonings by half.
- For soups and stews, double or triple all the ingredients, except for the liquid, seasonings, cornstarch and herbs.

Turkey Madeira

Rogene Rogers
Bemidji, MN

This is a wonderful, tasty and elegant dish served with a side of steamed baby carrots or broccoli with lemon butter.

1-1/2 lbs. turkey breast tenders
2-oz. pkg. dried mushrooms
3/4 c. chicken broth
1 T. lemon juice
3 T. Madeira wine or chicken
  broth

salt and pepper to taste
1 T. butter
2 t. cornstarch
cooked rice

In a slow cooker, layer all ingredients except butter, cornstarch and rice in order given. Cover and cook on low setting for 6 to 8 hours. To thicken sauce, melt butter in a saucepan over medium heat; stir in cornstarch. Add one cup cooking liquid. Bring to a boil; cook for 2 minutes, stirring constantly. Stir sauce back into slow cooker. Serve over cooked rice. Serves 4.

Creamy Italian Chicken

Jennifer Bontrager
Canton, MO

This is really good over brown rice.

8-oz. pkg. cream cheese, cubed
.7-oz. pkg. Italian salad
  dressing mix
1/2 c. water

4 boneless, skinless chicken
  breasts, cubed
cooked rice

Combine all ingredients except rice in a slow cooker; stir to mix. Cover and cook on low setting for 8 to 10 hours, or on high setting for 4 to 5 hours. Serve over rice. Makes about 4 servings.

Tex-Mex Chicken

Carla Hutto
Garrison, TX

*Try this with a sprinkling of chopped green onion and
a dollop of sour cream.*

5 to 6 boneless, skinless
chicken breasts
10-3/4 oz. can cream of
mushroom soup
10-3/4 oz. can cream of
chicken soup

10-oz. can tomatoes with chiles
corn chips
Garnish: shredded Cheddar
cheese

Place chicken in a slow cooker. Stir together soups and tomatoes; pour
over chicken. Cover and cook on low setting for 8 to 10 hours. Spoon
over corn chips; sprinkle with shredded cheese. Serves 4 to 6.

Anne's Chicken Burritos

Jennifer Sievers
Roselle, IL

*Anne is a friend of mine who gave me this easy slow-cooker recipe...
we love it more and more each time we make it!*

6 boneless, skinless chicken
breasts
15-1/4 oz. can corn, drained
16-oz. can black beans, drained
and rinsed

16-oz. jar salsa
6 to 8 10-inch flour tortillas
Garnish: shredded Cheddar
cheese, sour cream, salsa

Combine chicken, corn, beans and salsa in a slow cooker. Cover and
cook on low setting for 8 to 10 hours, or on high setting for 4 to
6 hours. Shred chicken; stir back into slow cooker. Roll up in tortillas;
garnish as desired. Serves 6 to 8.

Mexican Chicken

Stephanie Smith
Mansfield, TX

Turn up the heat with a garnish of sliced jalapeños!

15-oz. can black beans, drained
   and rinsed
2 15-1/4 oz. cans corn, drained
1 c. picante sauce, divided
2 lbs. boneless, skinless chicken
   breasts

Garnish: shredded Cheddar
   cheese
12 8-inch flour tortillas

Mix together beans, corn and 1/2 cup picante sauce in a slow cooker.
Place chicken on top; pour remaining picante sauce over chicken.
Cover and cook on high setting for 2-1/2 hours, or until chicken is
tender. Shred chicken and return to slow cooker. Sprinkle with cheese;
cover and cook until melted. Serve with tortillas. Serves 6.

Dress up the table in south-of-the-border style when serving
Mexican Chicken...arrange colorful woven blankets,
sombreros and tissue paper flowers around the room!

Maple-Glazed Turkey Breast

Vickie

Maple syrup and apricot preserves are the "secret" ingredients to this time-tested turkey recipe.

4 potatoes, peeled and cubed
1 onion, chopped
2-lb. boneless turkey breast
1/4 c. maple syrup

1/4 c. apricot preserves
Optional: 1/4 t. cinnamon
1/2 t. salt
1/8 t. pepper

Combine potatoes and onion in a slow cooker; place turkey breast on top. Combine remaining ingredients in a small bowl; mix well. Pour over turkey. Cover and cook on low setting for 6 to 7 hours, until vegetables are tender and turkey registers 180 degrees on a meat thermometer. Serves 4.

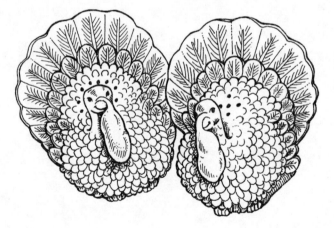

Don't serve turkey just on Thanksgiving! Turkey is scrumptious any time of year...use leftovers in a favorite chicken salad recipe or sliced over a chef salad.

Turkey & Mushroom Gravy

Robin Hill
Rochester, NY

*A dish that makes me feel like I'm back home...no matter how near
or far I happen to be.*

1 to 1-1/2 lbs. turkey breast
  tenders, halved
.87-oz. pkg. turkey gravy mix
10-3/4 oz. can cream of
  mushroom soup

1 T. onion-mushroom soup mix
4-oz. can sliced mushrooms,
  drained
salt and pepper to taste
cooked rice or mashed potatoes

Combine all ingredients except rice or potatoes in a slow cooker;
cover and cook on low setting for 6-1/2 to 8 hours. Serve over rice
or mashed potatoes. Serves 4.

Blend minced garlic, flavored cream cheese or shredded cheese
into warm mashed potatoes for a delicious side dish.

Chinese 5-Spice Chicken

Regina Wickline
Pebble Beach, CA

It's always been said that the Chinese 5-spice powder used in this recipe brings together 5 specific flavors...sour, bitter, sweet, pungent and salty. Give it a try...you'll be delighted!

1 stalk celery, sliced into
   1-inch pieces
3 green onions, sliced into
   1-inch pieces

4 to 5-lb. roasting chicken
1 T. soy sauce
2 t. Chinese 5-spice powder

Place celery and onions inside chicken. Combine soy sauce and spice powder to make a paste; rub over chicken. Place chicken in a slow cooker, on a rack, if desired. Cover and cook on low setting for 6 to 7 hours, until chicken is tender and juices run clear when pierced. Discard vegetables inside chicken; carve to serve. Serves 4.

Look for Chinese, South American or Italian music CD's at the local library...playing in the background during dinner, the music is a fun way to introduce the kids to something new!

Asian Chicken

Audrey Lett
Newark, DE

Serve in take-out containers...my family loves it!

3-1/2 lbs. boneless, skinless
   chicken breasts
1/3 c. peanut butter
2 T. soy sauce

3 T. orange juice
1/8 t. pepper
cooked rice or noodles

Place chicken in a slow cooker. Combine remaining ingredients except rice or noodles in a slow cooker; spread over chicken. Cover and cook on low setting for 6 to 8 hours, until chicken is tender. Serve with cooked rice or noodles. Serves 6.

Come on, try chopsticks when serving Asian Chicken!
Don't forget to pick up some fortune cookies too...sure to
make for a fun-filled dinner.

Chicken Cacciatore

Mary Whitacre
Mount Vernon, OH

I'm not that great of a cook, but every time I make this, my family just swoons! It is great any time of the year and is so easy.

1 lb. boneless, skinless chicken breasts
26-oz. jar chunky garden vegetable spaghetti sauce
1 zucchini, chopped
1 green pepper, chopped
1 sweet onion, chopped
cooked wide egg noodles or spaghetti
Garnish: chopped black olives, shredded Parmesan cheese

Place chicken in a slow cooker; pour sauce over top. Add vegetables. Cover and cook on low setting for 6 to 8 hours. Spoon over wide noodles or spaghetti. Garnish with black olives and Parmesan cheese. Serves 4.

When making a garden-fresh recipe like Chicken Cacciatore, use a mixture of veggies from the garden...just as tasty with any favorite combinations!

Garlic & Tomato Chicken

Ginger Brown
Ithaca, NY

Quick, easy and very tasty!

1 lb. boneless, skinless chicken
   breasts
2 15-oz. cans diced tomatoes
1 onion, chopped
1 clove garlic, minced

1 T. dried basil
salt and pepper to taste
1-1/4 c. water
cooked rotini pasta

Place chicken breasts in a slow cooker. Mix together remaining ingredients except rotini and pour over chicken. Cover and cook on low setting for 6 to 8 hours. Shred chicken with a fork; stir back into mixture in slow cooker. Serve over rotini. Serves 4 to 6.

Creamy Herbed Chicken

Cathy Neeley
North Logan, UT

Tender and moist with a touch of herbs and garlic.

4 boneless, skinless chicken
   breasts
10-3/4 oz. can cream of
   chicken with herbs soup
10-3/4 oz. can cream of
   mushroom with roasted
   garlic soup

1.2-oz. pkg. savory garlic &
   herb soup mix
2/3 c. water
cooked rice or noodles

Place chicken in a slow cooker. Combine soups, soup mix and water; pour over top. Cover and cook chicken on low setting for 6 to 8 hours, or on high setting for 3 to 4 hours. Serve over rice or noodles. Serves 4.

Just Peachy Chicken

Elizabeth Blackstone
Racine, WI

Try substituting apricot preserves too...scrumptious!

4 boneless, skinless chicken thighs
2 sweet potatoes, peeled and cubed

1 onion, chopped
2 T. cold water
3 T. cornstarch
1/2 c. peach preserves

Place chicken in a slow cooker; add sweet potatoes and onion. Cover and cook on low setting for 7 to 8 hours. Pour off juices from slow cooker into a saucepan; set aside. Cover chicken, sweet potatoes and onion to keep warm. In a heavy saucepan, combine water and cornstarch; mix well. Add reserved juices from slow cooker; stir in preserves. Cook and stir over medium heat, stirring frequently, until mixture boils and thickens. Cook for 2 minutes; pour over chicken and vegetables. Serves 4.

Keep salad tossing simple...add ingredients to a plastic zipping bag, seal, then shake!

Apple-Stuffed Turkey Breast

Dale Duncan
Waterloo, IA

The combination of wild rice, apples and cranberries really give this turkey an amazing flavor.

1-1/2 c. wild rice, uncooked
2 apples, cored, peeled and
  chopped
1 onion, finely chopped
1/2 c. sweetened, dried
  cranberries

3 c. water
4 to 5-lb. boneless, skinless
  turkey breast

Combine rice, apples, onion and cranberries in a slow cooker; pour water over top. Mix well. Place turkey on top of rice mixture. Cover and cook on low setting for 8 to 9 hours. Serves 10.

Burstin' with Berries Turkey

April Jacobs
Loveland, CO

Cranberries and turkey just seem to go together, and in this recipe, they make a winning combination

2 lbs. turkey breast tenders
1/3 c. orange juice
3/4 c. whole-berry cranberry
  sauce
2 T. brown sugar, packed

1 T. soy sauce
salt and pepper to taste
Optional: 1/2 t. allspice
1 T. cold water
1 T. cornstarch

Combine all ingredients except water and cornstarch in a slow cooker; turn turkey to coat. Cover and cook on low setting for 7 to 9 hours, or on high setting for 3-1/2 to 4 hours. About 10 minutes before serving, stir together cold water and cornstarch; add to turkey mixture. Cover and cook until thickened, about 10 minutes. Sprinkle with additional salt and pepper. Serves 4.

Charlene's Ritzy Chicken

Dottie Croyle
Perry, OH

Nothing says comfort food like a chicken and mashed potatoes meal.

10-3/4 oz. can cream of
  chicken soup
1 pt. sour cream
1 sleeve round buttery crackers,
  crushed

1/2 c. butter, melted
4 to 6 boneless, skinless
  chicken breasts
mashed potatoes

Combine soup and sour cream in a small bowl; set aside. In a separate bowl, mix together crackers and butter. Place chicken in a slow cooker; spoon soup mixture over top and sprinkle with cracker mixture. Cover and cook on low setting for 7 to 9 hours, or on high setting for 4 to 5 hours. Serve over mashed potatoes. Serves 4 to 6.

Vintage buttons, metal pop bottle lids, typewriter keys and dice all make for clever refrigerator magnets. Add a bit of hot glue and secure a magnet dot on the back...so easy!

Mozzarella Chicken & Rice

Jennifer Martineau
Gooseberry Patch

Dress this up with anything you like...mushrooms, black olives and garlic all add terrific flavor.

8 boneless, skinless chicken
   breasts
1/4 t. salt
1/8 t. pepper
1 onion, chopped

2 green peppers, coarsely
   chopped
2 c. pasta sauce
1 c. shredded mozzarella cheese
cooked orzo pasta or rice

Place chicken in a slow cooker; sprinkle with salt and pepper. Top with onion and green peppers; pour pasta sauce over top. Cover and cook on low setting for 4 to 5 hours. Stir well and sprinkle with cheese. Let stand for 5 minutes, until cheese is melted. Serve over cooked pasta or rice. Serves 8.

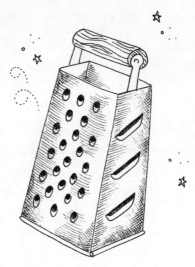

Pick up old-fashioned box graters or minnow buckets at auctions and tag sales...with a votive slipped underneath, they'll cast a delightful flickering glow across the dinner table.

27

Chicken Italiano

Tina Wright
Atlanta, GA

You could add vegetables to this recipe to make it a one-dish meal.
Baby carrots or chopped onion go under the chicken, while sliced
mushrooms, peppers and zucchini can be tossed in during the last
hour of cooking.

2 lbs. boneless, skinless chicken
    breasts, cut into strips
1/4 c. butter, melted
8-oz. container cream cheese
    with chives, softened
10-3/4 oz. can golden
    mushroom soup

.7 oz. pkg. Italian salad
    dressing mix
1/2 c. water
cooked bowtie pasta or rice

Place chicken in a slow cooker; set aside. In a medium bowl, combine
melted butter, cream cheese, soup, dressing mix and water in a bowl;
stir until blended and pour over chicken. Cover and cook on low
setting for 6 to 8 hours. Stir well; serve over cooked pasta or rice.
Serves 4 to 6.

It's always best to fluff rice with a fork after cooking instead of
stirring with a spoon...with a fork it's sure to be fluffy every time!

Oriental Chicken

Sherry Gordon
Arlington Heights, IL

*A garnish of minced chives is tasty on servings of this
sweet-and-sour chicken.*

2 lbs. boneless, skinless
  chicken thighs, cut into
  bite-size pieces
2 12-oz. jars sweet-and-
  sour sauce

16-oz. pkg. frozen broccoli,
  carrots and peppers blend,
  thawed and drained

Combine chicken and sauce in a slow cooker. Cover and cook on low
setting for 7 to 8 hours. Shortly before serving, stir in vegetables.
Increase to high setting; cover and cook for 10 to 15 minutes, until
vegetables are crisp-tender. Serves 6 to 8.

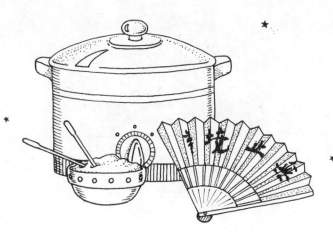

For easy, no-fuss cleaning, just fill an empty slow cooker
with warm, soapy water and let soak.

Super-Simple Chicken Dinner

Rachel Rivas
Menifee, CA

*Ready in only 4 hours, this will be a constant meal
on your family table.*

4 boneless, skinless chicken breasts	1/2 c. water
	1/2 t. salt
26-oz. jar spaghetti sauce	cooked egg noodles

Place chicken in a slow cooker; add sauce, water and salt. Cover and cook on high setting for 4 hours. Spoon shredded chicken and sauce over cooked noodles. Serves 4.

When a recipe calls for spaghetti sauce, try something new
each time. With so many choices at your grocery store,
try swapping out your usual sauce for tomato-basil,
roasted red pepper or garlic & herb.

Debbie's Cheesy Chicken

Debbie Anderson
Lafayette, IN

*Try substituting a can of nacho cheese soup for the Cheddar...
an easy way to add a new twist to this recipe.*

6 boneless, skinless chicken
   breasts
garlic powder to taste
salt and pepper to taste
2 10-3/4 oz. cans cream of
   chicken soup

10-3/4 oz. can Cheddar cheese
   soup
cooked rice or noodles

Place chicken in a slow cooker; sprinkle with garlic powder, salt and pepper. Mix together soups and pour over chicken. Cover and cook on low setting for 6 to 8 hours. Serve over rice or noodles. Serves 6.

Crunchy veggies make a nice go-with at dinnertime...just for fun,
serve veggie dip in a hollowed-out round loaf of bread.

Mom's Company Chicken

Amanda Homan
Gooseberry Patch

The flavors come together to make this chicken dish one I serve again and again...to rave reviews!

2 lbs. boneless, skinless chicken
   thighs
3 cloves garlic, minced
1 onion, chopped

1/2 c. sweet-and-sour sauce
1/2 c. barbecue sauce
cooked rice or couscous

Combine all ingredients except rice or couscous in a slow cooker. Cover and cook on low setting for 8 to 9 hours, until chicken is cooked through. Serve over cooked rice or couscous. Serves 6.

Kitchen string comes in handy so many times...so when you need to use it, remember this handy tip. Place the ball of string inside a small pan. As you pull on the string, the ball rolls around inside the pan instead of all over the counter and floor!

Sweet & Spicy Chicken

Annette Ingram
Grand Rapids, MI

*The sweetness of the marmalade blends with the curry and cayenne to
make one amazing slow-cooker chicken!*

4 to 6 boneless, skinless
   chicken breasts
salt and pepper to taste
12-oz. jar orange marmalade

1/2 c. chicken broth
1-1/2 t. curry powder
1/2 t. cayenne pepper
Optional: 1/8 t. ground ginger

Sprinkle chicken with salt and pepper; place in a slow cooker. In a
bowl, whisk together marmalade, broth and spices. Pour over
chicken. Cover and cook on low setting for 5 to 7 hours, or on high
setting for 3 to 4 hours, turning chicken halfway through cooking.
Serves 4 to 6.

Make herbed butter to serve with dinner in a jiffy...just roll a
stick of butter in freshly chopped herbs, slice and serve!

Chicken Swiss Supreme

Lynn Williams
Muncie, IN

*One of my all-time favorites to serve when we have friends over
for Sunday dinner.*

3 slices bacon, crisply cooked,
   crumbled and drippings
   reserved
6 boneless, skinless chicken
   breasts

4-oz. can sliced mushrooms,
   drained
10-3/4 oz. can cream of
   chicken soup
1/2 c. Swiss cheese, diced

In a skillet over medium heat, cook chicken in reserved bacon
drippings for 3 to 5 minutes, until lightly golden, turning once. Place
chicken in a slow cooker; top with mushrooms. Stir soup into skillet;
heat through and pour over chicken. Cover and cook on low setting
for 4 to 5 hours, until chicken is cooked through. Top chicken with
cheese and sprinkle with bacon. Cover and cook on high setting
for 10 to 15 minutes, or until cheese is melted. Makes 6 servings.

If there seems to be a bit too much liquid inside the slow cooker,
and it's almost dinnertime, tilt the lid and turn the slow cooker
to its high setting...soon the liquid will begin to evaporate.

Beef

Louisiana-Style Pot Roast

Teri Naquin
Melville, LA

The onion soup makes this pot roast taste so good, and using the slow cooker makes the meat very moist. I gave this recipe to a friend in a recipe swap, and she told me her family really enjoyed it.

4-lb. beef chuck roast
salt and pepper to taste
2 T. oil
1.35-oz. pkg. onion soup mix
1 c. water

3 carrots, peeled and chopped
1 onion, chopped
3 potatoes, peeled and cubed
Optional: 1 stalk celery, chopped

Sprinkle roast with salt and pepper. In a large skillet over medium-high heat, brown roast in oil on all sides; place in a slow cooker. Add remaining ingredients. Cover and cook on low setting for 8 to 10 hours. Makes 6 to 8 servings.

Enjoy an autumn dinner under the trees...just tote a slow-cooker dinner out to a harvest table. Arrange hay bales around the table for easy seating.

Corned Beef & Cabbage

Ethel Peris
Millersville, PA

This traditional dish is super-easy to make in the slow cooker.

1 c. water
6 to 7 potatoes, peeled and
   quartered

1 head cabbage, quartered and
   leaves separated
12-oz. can corned beef, sliced

Pour water into a slow cooker. Layer remaining ingredients in order given. Cover and cook on low setting for 6 to 8 hours. Makes 4 servings.

A rainy day cure-all...toss together all the ingredients
for a tasty slower-cooker meal, make some popcorn
and enjoy a classic movie marathon. When you're
ready for dinner, it's ready for you!

Spicy Tortellini & Meatballs

Jennifer Vallimont
Kersey, PA

This has to be one of my favorites for the slow cooker because it cooks for such a short time. When I don't have meatballs in the freezer, I have substituted browned and drained ground beef for the meatballs and it's just as tasty.

14-oz. pkg. frozen cooked
    Italian meatballs, thawed
16-oz. pkg. frozen broccoli,
    cauliflower and carrot blend,
    thawed
2 c. cheese tortellini, uncooked

2 10-3/4 oz. cans cream of
    mushroom soup
2-1/4 c. water
1/2 to 1 t. ground cumin
salt and pepper to taste

Combine meatballs, vegetables and tortellini in a slow cooker. In a large bowl, whisk together soup, water and seasonings. Pour over meatball mixture; stir to combine well. Cover and cook on low setting for 3 to 4 hours. Makes 6 to 8 servings.

If it's a warm spring or summer day, consider enjoying
Spicy Tortellini & Meatballs outside...Italian style! Set the table
with touches of green, white and red...the colors of
the Italian flag are ideal paired with bunches of grapes
and Italian music playing in the background.

Italian Beef & Pasta

Evelyn Webb
Chicago Heights, IL

*Two meals in one, because any leftovers make great sandwiches
the next day!*

3 to 4-lb. beef chuck roast
2 onions, sliced
13-1/4 oz. can sliced mushrooms
2 26-oz. jars marinara pasta
   sauce

2 T. zesty Italian salad dressing
   mix
16-oz. pkg. spaghetti, cooked

Combine all ingredients except spaghetti in a slow cooker. Cover and cook on low setting for 8 hours. Slice beef; spoon sauce over cooked pasta and serve beef on the side. Serves 8 to 10.

When making this week's shopping list, don't forget to add
a bouquet of flowers...so cheery!

Creamy Beef Stroganoff

Shelly Smith
Dana, IN

A midwestern favorite!

2 lbs. stew beef, cubed
salt and pepper to taste
2 10-3/4 oz. cans cream of
  mushroom soup

3 T. Worcestershire sauce
3-oz. pkg. cream cheese, cubed
16-oz. container sour cream
cooked rice or noodles

Place beef in a slow cooker; sprinkle with salt and pepper. Pour soup over top; add Worcestershire sauce. Cover and cook on low setting for 8 to 10 hours. Stir in cream cheese and sour cream 30 minutes before serving. Serve over rice or noodles. Serves 6 to 8.

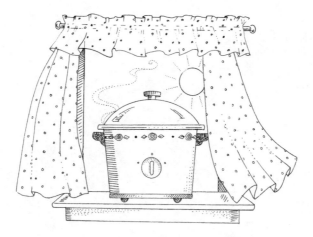

When spring cleaning time rolls around, slow-cooker dishes make mealtime a breeze. Add all the ingredients, turn it on and forget about it. Now, throw open the windows and air out the quilts with no worries about what's for dinner!

Beef Tips & Gravy

Kathleen White
Cato, NY

All ten members of my family raved about this slow-cooker creation.

3 lbs. stew beef, cubed
15-oz. can tomato sauce
2 c. water
1.35-oz. pkg. onion soup mix

1/3 c. instant tapioca, uncooked
1 to 2 t. beef bouillon granules
cooked egg noodles

Place beef in a slow cooker. Combine remaining ingredients except noodles; pour over beef. Cover and cook on low setting for 8 to 10 hours, or on high setting for 5 to 6 hours. Serve over cooked noodles. Serves 6 to 8.

When preparing a recipe with lots of fresh veggies, save time by visiting the salad bar at your local grocery store. Buy only what you need of freshly-chopped carrots, broccoli and cauliflower flowerets or sliced onions.

Mom's Black-Eyed Pea Soup

Dana Cunningham
Lafayette, LA

This is one recipe sure to be found in every recipe box in our family.

16-oz. pkg. dried black-eyed
  peas
10-3/4 oz. can bean with bacon
  soup

4 c. water
6 carrots, peeled and chopped
2-lb. beef chuck roast, cubed
1/4 t. pepper

Combine all ingredients in a slow cooker; mix well. Cover and cook on low setting for 9 to 10 hours. Makes 6 servings.

When serving rolls alongside soup, try topping them with tangy Lemon-Parsley Butter...it's so easy to make. Simply blend together 1/2 cup butter with salt and white pepper to taste, then stir in 2 tablespoons lemon juice. Wrap 3 tablespoons chopped parsley in a paper towel, to remove the moisture, then add to the butter mixture.

Montana Wild Rice Beef Stew

Rhonda Reeder
Ellicott City, MD

Our family stayed in a rustic cabin on our autumn trip to Montana one year, and a big bowl of this soup warmed us up head-to-toe on those chilly evenings around the campfire.

4 c. sliced mushrooms
3 carrots, peeled and sliced
   1/2-inch thick
6-oz. pkg. long-grain and wild
   rice

1 lb. beef sirloin, cubed
5 c. beef broth

Combine mushrooms, carrots and rice mix with seasoning packet in a slow cooker. Top with beef; pour broth over top. Cover and cook on low setting for 8 to 10 hours. Serves 6.

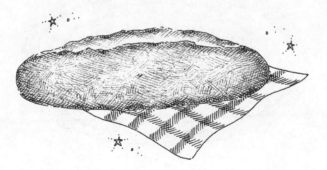

For flavorful, fast-fix bread to serve with soups, simply brush Italian bread slices with butter. Sprinkle on garlic & herb seasoning blend and broil until golden.

Teriyaki Beef

Molly Cool
Gooseberry Patch

With only 3 ingredients, this is the recipe I reach for when I find time's short!

1/3 c. teriyaki marinade
8-oz. can crushed pineapple

1-1/2 lb. boneless beef chuck
  steak

Spray a slow cooker with non-stick vegetable spray; add marinade and pineapple with juice. Place steak in marinade mixture. Cover and cook on high setting for 2-1/2 to 3-1/2 hours. Makes 4 servings.

Every house where love abides and friendship is a guest
is surely home, and home sweet home;
for there the heart can rest.

-Henry Van Dyke

Super-Easy Slow-Cooker Roast

Lynn Smith
Little Rock, AR

*My son and daughter love this roast because it makes a delicious
gravy that is so good spooned over mashed potatoes or rice.*

3-1/2 lb. beef pot roast
1.35-oz. pkg. onion soup mix
26-oz. can cream of mushroom
  soup

1-2/3 c. water

Place pot roast in slow cooker; sprinkle with soup mix. Pour soup over
top; add water. Cover and cook on low setting for 8 to 10 hours, or on
high setting for 4 to 6 hours. Serves 4 to 6.

Remember that long, slow cooking is ideal for inexpensive
cuts of meat because it provides plenty of time
for tenderizing the meat.

Magic Meatloaf

Pat Prater
Munford, TN

It's magic the way this cooks up...so delicious and moist. Try it sliced on sandwiches for the next day's lunch.

2 lbs. ground beef
2 eggs, beaten
1 c. quick-cooking oats,
    uncooked

1/2 c. catsup
1-1/2 c. mild salsa

Combine ground beef, eggs, oats, catsup and salsa. Shape into a loaf. Place in a slow cooker. Cover and cook on low setting for 8 to 10 hours, or on high setting for 4 to 6 hours. Serves 4 to 6.

Host a potluck dinner with neighbors..only slow cookers
allowed! You'll be amazed at what a variety of
tasty meals will arrive.

Homestyle Stuffed Peppers

Carolyn Russell
Clyde, NC

My great-grandmother taught me how to cook, sew, crochet and quilt. One of the things I remember most is how she would have supper ready for me when I lived near her. She knew I loved green peppers and she would always fix them for me. When I wanted to make them for my children, I created this quick-to-fix recipe for the slow cooker so my kids could have great food like I grew up on.

1-1/2 lbs. ground beef
1 onion, finely chopped
1 c. instant rice, uncooked
4 green peppers, tops removed

15-oz. can tomato sauce
Optional: salt-free seasoning
  to taste

Mix together ground beef, onion and rice; spoon into peppers. Arrange peppers in a slow cooker; pour tomato sauce over top. Sprinkle with seasoning, if desired. Cover and cook on low setting for 5 to 6 hours. Serves 4.

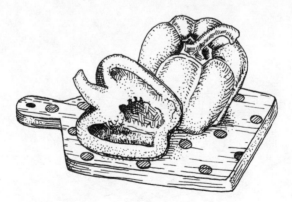

Green peppers are so versatile...stuff them with shrimp, ground beef and rice, ham & cheese or Italian sausage.

Tangy Beef & Noodles

Lisa Ashton
Aston, PA

*There are so many flavors of barbecue sauce...from traditional tomato
to fruit, mustard and vinegar. Try something new for a change
each time you make this.*

2 to 2-1/2 lbs. stew beef, cubed
1 c. barbecue sauce
1 T. prepared horseradish
1 t. mustard
1/4 t. salt
1/8 t. pepper
cooked wide egg noodles

Place beef in a slow cooker. Combine barbecue sauce, horseradish,
mustard, salt and pepper in a small bowl; pour over beef. Cover and
cook on low setting for 7 to 8 hours. Arrange meat and sauce over
noodles. Serves 4 to 6.

Tangy Beef & Noodles is a backyard get-together favorite.
Dress up the picnic table...just tie a bouquet of balloons to a
bucket filled with bottles of icy root beer and red pop.

Sandra's Slow-Cooker Brisket

Sandra Lee Smith
Arleta, CA

I grew up in a large family and we always enjoyed a lot of one-dish meals. This was before slow cookers came along, so most of my mother's favorite recipes have been converted to use in the slow cooker. I like my slow cookers so much, I have them in 3 different sizes!

1 onion, sliced
3 to 4-lb. beef brisket
1 T. smoke-flavored cooking
   sauce

12-oz. bottle chili sauce
salt and pepper to taste

Arrange onion slices in a slow cooker; place brisket on top of onion. Add smoke-flavored cooking sauce; pour chili sauce over brisket. Sprinkle with salt and pepper. Cover and cook on low setting for 10 to 12 hours. Makes 6 servings.

A garden-fresh side dish that's ready in a jiffy. Beat together one cup sour cream, 2 tablespoons vinegar and 4 tablespoons sugar. Fold in one peeled and thinly sliced cucumber; add salt and pepper to taste.

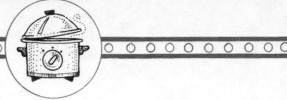

Chuck Wagon Stew

Peggy Pelfrey
Fort Riley, KS

This hearty stew would be ideal for a fall social or weekend at the cabin.

1-1/2 lbs. stew beef, cubed
1/2 lb. smoked sausage, sliced
1 onion, chopped

3 potatoes, cubed
28-oz. can barbecue baked beans

Place beef, sausage, onion and potatoes into a slow cooker; mix well. Spoon baked beans over top. Cover and cook on low setting for 8 to 10 hours, or cook on high setting 4 to 5 hours. Makes 6 servings.

Serve up Chuck Wagon Stew cowboy style. Spoon stew into enamelware bowls, add a side of cornbread and keep bandannas on hand for terrific lap-size napkins.

Slow-Cooked Beef Tips

Lisa Hartz
Washington, IN

An elegant dish that everyone loves.

1 lb. beef tips
10-3/4 oz. can cream of
   mushroom soup
1-oz. pkg. onion soup mix

1 c. lemon-lime soda
1/2 c. green peppers, chopped
cooked egg noodles

Spray a slow cooker with non-stick vegetable spray. Add all ingredients except noodles; mix well. Cover and cook on low setting for 6 to 8 hours. Serve over noodles. Makes 6 servings.

Spoon soups and stews into hollowed-out pumpkins that are anything but ordinary. Pumpkins can be found in lots of colors...Long Island Cheese is tan, while Jarrahdale is blue-gray. Valenciano pumpkins are snow white and Kakai are orange with black stripes.

Fall-Apart Roast Beef with Coffee

JoAnn

Coffee adds a unique flavor to a traditional recipe. You can also rub the roast with minced garlic and sprinkle with onion powder if you'd like.

4-lb. beef chuck roast
5 cloves garlic
1-1/2 c. hot brewed coffee

1/2 c. cold water
2 T. cornstarch

Using a sharp knife, make 5 deep slits around top and side of roast. Push the whole cloves of garlic into the slits. Place roast in a slow cooker; pour coffee over top. Cover and cook on low setting for 6 to 8 hours. Remove from slow cooker; pour juices into a small saucepan over medium heat. In a small bowl, combine water and cornstarch; mix well. Slowly add to juices, stirring constantly. Simmer until thickened, about 3 to 5 minutes, and spoon over servings. Serves 4 to 6.

Sprigs of rosemary and cherry tomatoes make an oh-so-pretty garnish for any dinner plate.

Slow-Cooker Swiss Steak

*Cathy Callen
Lawton, OK*

Ready-made mashed potatoes from the grocer's make an ideal side with this dinner...they're ready in 5 minutes and taste like homemade.

1-lb. beef round steak, cut into
   serving-size pieces
salt and pepper to taste

1.35-oz. pkg. onion soup mix
16-oz. can stewed tomatoes

Sprinkle steak with salt and pepper; place in a slow cooker. Add remaining ingredients. Cover and cook on low setting for 6 to 8 hours, or on high setting for 3 to 4 hours. Makes 4 servings.

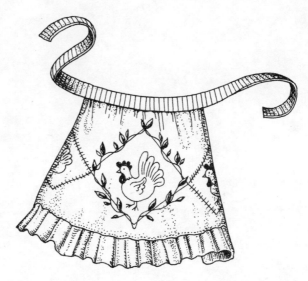

Revive the apron-wearing tradition! Look through flea markets for some of the prettiest patterns and fabrics, or find a fun pattern and stitch one up in an afternoon.

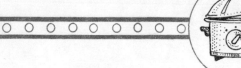

Cajun Pot Roast

Kerry Mayer
Dunham Springs, LA

A flavorful roast that's savory and delicious.

2-lb. boneless beef chuck roast
1 T. Cajun seasoning
1 onion, chopped
14-1/2 oz. can diced tomatoes
    with garlic

1/2 t. hot pepper sauce
1/8 t. pepper

Sprinkle roast with Cajun seasoning; rub to coat. Place roast in a slow cooker; top with onion. Combine remaining ingredients; pour over roast. Cover and cook on low setting for 8 to 10 hours. Serves 6.

Vintage lunchboxes can hold all kinds of necessities when you're traveling on-the-road. Filled with napkins, straws, maps, coins and tissue packets, a lunchbox is a handy way to hold all those little indispensables!

Sally's Supreme Corned Beef

Sally Kohler
Webster, NY

Use a little cornstarch to thicken the broth after removing the brisket...
it makes really good gravy for the noodles.

2 to 3-lb. corned beef brisket
12-oz. bottle chili sauce
1.35-oz. pkg. onion soup mix

12-oz. can cola
cooked egg noodles

Place brisket in slow cooker. Mix remaining ingredients except noodles; pour over brisket. Cover and cook on low setting and cook for 6 to 8 hours. Slice beef and serve over noodles. Makes 4 to 6 servings.

If you're making Sally's Supreme Corned Beef for St. Patrick's Day, add some Irish whimsies when setting the table. Toss gold foil-covered chocolate coins around place settings, add a touch o' green with a shamrock plant centerpiece and play traditional Irish music during dinner.

Texas Beef Chili

Connie Hilty
Pearland, TX

So easy to prepare, this long-simmering chili is the best I've ever tasted.

2 lbs. stew beef, cubed
1 onion, chopped
15-oz. can chunky tomato sauce

12-oz. jar thick and chunky
   salsa
1 green pepper, chopped

Combine all ingredients except green pepper in a slow cooker. Cover and cook on low setting for 8 to 10 hours. Stir in pepper; increase to high setting and cook for an additional 15 to 20 minutes. Serves 6.

Tuck silverware and napkins into
new fleece caps or mittens...
everyone gets something new
for the winter days ahead,
and it's a fun-filled way to set
the table on a frosty day.

Pasta Fagioli Soup

Susie Kadleck
San Antonio, TX

*A crispy salad and bread sticks served alongside and you'll feel
like you're at a favorite Italian restaurant!*

1 lb. ground beef, browned and
   drained
18.8-oz. can minestrone soup

10-oz. can tomatoes with chiles
16-oz. can pinto or kidney
   beans, drained and rinsed

Combine all ingredients in a slow cooker. Cover and cook on low
setting for 2 to 3 hours. Makes 4 servings.

Light candles for a soft glow at dinnertime. In the summer,
nestle votives in jars filled with sand and tiny shells...in fall,
tuck them into hollowed-out apples.

Pine Cones in Tomato Sauce

Lisa Ashton
Aston, PA

No, they're not really pine cones, but tasty beef and rice balls.

2 8-oz. cans tomato sauce	1/2 c. long-cooking rice
1/4 t. garlic powder	2 T. onion, chopped
1/2 c. water	1/2 t. salt
1-1/4 lbs. ground beef	1/4 t. pepper

Mix together tomato sauce, garlic powder and water in a slow cooker. Combine remaining ingredients in a large bowl; mix well. Shape into 24 pine cone-shaped balls; arrange in slow cooker. Cover and cook on low setting for 7 to 8 hours. Makes 4 servings.

Long-cooking rice is best for slow-cooker recipes...it stays firm, while instant rice can overcook and become mushy.

Midwestern Goulash

Jane Dellinger
Peoria, IL

I received this recipe from my aunt, a very good cook who used the slow cooker often. Everyone who has had this agrees...it's delicious!

2 to 2-1/2 lb. beef roast, cubed
salt and pepper to taste
1 slice bacon, chopped

1 onion, chopped
14-oz. bottle catsup
cooked egg noodles

Combine all ingredients except noodles in a slow cooker. Cover and cook on low setting for 8 to 10 hours. Serve over noodles. Makes 4 servings.

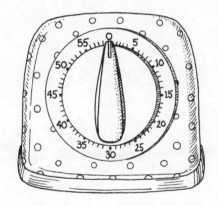

When slow cooking at higher altitudes, recipes tend to take a bit longer. Add an extra 30 minutes of cooking time to each hour in a recipe.

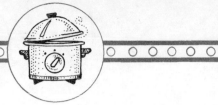

Savory Pot Roast

Carol Tootalian
Troy, MI

*Best roast I have ever had...the gravy is so tasty. The first time I made
this my kids were very impressed.*

3-1/2 lb. beef chuck roast
1-oz. pkg. ranch salad dressing
   mix

1.35-oz. pkg. onion soup mix
.87-oz. pkg. brown gravy mix
1/2 c. warm water

Place roast in a slow cooker. Mix dry ingredients together and sprinkle
over roast. Pour water into slow cooker around roast. Cover and cook
on low setting for 6 to 7 hours. Makes 6 servings.

When traveling in an RV, slow cookers can't be beat! As they
cook away, you're free to enjoy the scenery, shop for souvenirs
or stop at barn sales and flea markets discovered along the way.

Beefy Mushroom Bake

Claire Bertram
Lexington, KY

Quick-cooking barley is a terrific pantry staple, and is so tasty in this slow-cooked dinner.

1 to 1-1/2 lbs. beef round steak, cubed
3/4 c. quick-cooking barley, uncooked

10-3/4 oz. can golden mushroom soup
2/3 c. water
3/4 lb. sliced mushrooms

Combine all ingredients in a slow cooker; mix well. Cover and cook on low setting for 7 to 8 hours. Serves 4 to 6.

Make a scrapbook of Mom's favorite recipes...just going through the recipe box together will stir up sweet memories. Once favorite recipes are chosen, make copies and add family photos. Taken to the nearest copy shop, extras of the scrapbook can quickly and easily be made to share with family & friends.

So-Easy Slow-Cooker Pot Roast

Hilary Stubblebine
Delaware, OH

One dinner you'll love coming home to.

3 to 4-lb. beef chuck roast
10-3/4 oz. can tomato soup
10-3/4 oz. can cream of
   mushroom soup

2 16-oz. cans new potatoes,
   drained
2 14-1/2 oz. cans sliced carrots,
   drained

Mix together all ingredients in a slow cooker. Cover and cook on low setting for 7 to 8 hours. Serves 6.

To make clean-up a breeze, lightly spray the inside of
a slow cooker with non-stick vegetable spray, then add
recipe ingredients. What a time-saver!

Baja Steak

Geneva Rogers
Gillette, WY

*The steak is so tender, turn any leftovers into amazing beef burritos
for a cook-once, eat-twice dinner.*

1-1/2 lbs. boneless beef round
steak, cut into serving-size
pieces
2 c. frozen corn, thawed and
drained
18-oz. jar chunky garden salsa

15-oz. can black beans, drained
and rinsed
1 onion, chopped
1/2 c. water
1/2 t. salt
Optional: 1/8 t. red pepper flakes

Place beef in a slow cooker. Mix remaining ingredients together; pour
over beef. Cover and cook on low setting for 8 to 9 hours. Serves 6.

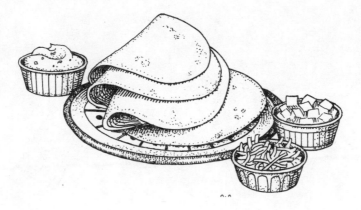

It's so easy to turn leftover beef or pork roasts into the best-
tasting burritos. Warm tortillas by heating them one at a time in
a large skillet over medium heat, flipping when they begin to puff.
Remove from heat and spread a portion of warm beef or pork
on each tortilla; add rice, sour cream, guacamole and pico
de gallo or salsa to taste. Roll up and serve...delicious!

Smokey Beef Brisket

Rita Morgan
Pueblo, CO

Tender slices of brisket with an amazing flavor.

2-1/2 lb. beef brisket, halved
1 T. smoke-flavored cooking
   sauce
1 t. salt
1/2 t. pepper

1/2 c. onion, chopped
1/2 c. catsup
2 t. Dijon mustard
1/2 t. celery seed

Rub brisket with smoke-flavored cooking sauce, salt and pepper; place in a slow cooker. Top with onion. Combine remaining ingredients; spread over brisket. Cover and cook on low setting for 8 to 9 hours. Remove brisket and keep warm. Transfer cooking juices to a blender; process until smooth. Serve with brisket. Serves 4 to 6.

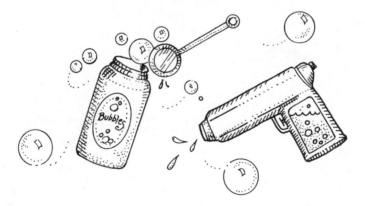

While dinner's cookin' away, enjoy playing with the kids outside. Did you know you can catch a bubble in your hands if your hands are wet? Try it...the kids will giggle!

Cola Roast

Wendy Hall
East Canton, OH

A tried & true family favorite. Always remember when preparing this recipe, not to use diet cola.

3-lb. beef pot roast
1.35-oz. pkg. onion soup mix

2 12-oz. cans cola

Place roast in a slow cooker; sprinkle with soup mix. Pour cola over top. Cover and cook on low setting for 7 to 8 hours. Makes 8 to 10 servings.

Serve up a slow-cooker dinner under a shady tree or on a sunny hillside...a terrific way to kick back and enjoy family time together.

Spaghetti & Meatballs

Susie Backus
Gooseberry Patch

Perfect pairing with a fresh green salad from your garden patch.

1 lb. frozen cooked meatballs,
  thawed
26-oz. jar spaghetti sauce
1 onion, chopped
1-1/2 c. water

8-oz. pkg. spaghetti, uncooked
  and broken into 3-inch
  pieces
Garnish: grated Parmesan
  cheese

Combine meatballs, spaghetti sauce, onion and water in a slow cooker. Cover and cook on low setting for 6 to 8 hours. Stir well; add broken spaghetti. Increase to high setting; cover and cook for an additional hour, stirring once during cooking. Serve with Parmesan cheese. Serves 4 to 6.

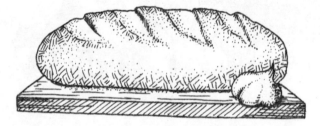

Savory garlic bread...so easy to make at home. Blend together
1/2 cup softened butter with one tablespoon chopped parsley,
2 minced garlic cloves and 1/4 cup freshly grated Parmesan
cheese. Spread over Italian bread halves, broil 2 to 3 minutes
until edges become golden and cheese bubbles.
Slice and serve...mmm!

Pork

Autumn Pork Roast

Vickie

*Apple cider is the must-use ingredient to make the most tender
pork roast you'll ever taste.*

2-lb. boneless pork loin roast
3/4 t. salt
1/4 t. pepper
2 c. apple cider, divided

3 sprigs fresh rosemary, divided
1/2 c. sweetened, dried cherries
5 t. cornstarch

Sprinkle roast with salt and pepper; place in a non-stick skillet coated
with non-stick vegetable spray. Brown roast over medium heat for
about 4 minutes per side. Pour one cup apple cider into a slow cooker.
Add 2 sprigs rosemary; top with roast and remaining rosemary.
Sprinkle cherries around roast. Cover and cook on low setting for
5 to 6 hours, or until a meat thermometer reads 160 degrees. Remove
roast; keep warm. Strain cooking juices into a small saucepan. Stir in
3/4 cup cider; bring to a boil over medium heat. Combine remaining
cider and cornstarch until smooth. Gradually whisk into cider mixture.
Bring to a boil; cook and stir for one to 2 minutes, until thickened.
Serve over roast. Makes 6 servings.

Applesauce just seems
made to go with any
pork dinner. Sprinkle
applesauce servings
with a little apple pie
spice or drizzle with
a bit of honey for
even more flavor.

Dad's Pork Tenderloin

Jason Keller
Carrollton, GA

Dad whipped up this very simple recipe one weekend years ago.
The pork comes out so tender...the meat just falls apart.

2 1-lb. pork tenderloins
10-3/4 oz. can cream of
  mushroom soup
10-3/4 oz. can golden
  mushroom soup

10-1/2 oz. can French onion
  soup
Optional: mashed potatoes

Place pork in a slow cooker. Combine soups in a bowl; stir until smooth and pour over pork. Cover and cook on low for 4 to 5 hours, or until meat is tender. Serve with mashed potatoes, if desired. Serves 6.

Look for small vintage salt & pepper shakers at tag sales...it's so much fun to set a pair at each place setting.

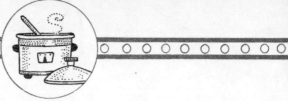

French Onion Pork Chops

Rebecca Ruff
Carthage, NY

Pork chops and apples pair up nicely...spoon some old-fashioned fried apples into bowls for an easy side dish.

4 pork chops
10-1/2 oz. can French onion
  soup

1/4 c. water
1 t. dried parsley
cooked egg noodles

Place pork chops in a slow cooker. Mix soup and water together; pour over pork. Sprinkle with parsley. Cover and cook on low for about 8 hours. Serve over hot cooked noodles. Serves 4.

Yummy Pork & Gravy

Cindy Sullivan
Shelbyville, TN

While rice is a good go-with for these pork chops too, cornbread makes a really tasty change.

6 boneless pork chops, cut into
  bite-size pieces
2 10-3/4 oz. cans cream of
  mushroom soup
6-oz. can French fried onions

2 stalks celery, chopped
1-1/4 c. milk
1-1/2 t. salt
1 t. pepper
cornbread

Combine all ingredients except cornbread in a slow cooker; mix well. Cover and cook on low setting for 6 hours, or on high setting for 4 hours. Serve over cornbread. Makes 8 servings.

Pork Chops & Scalloped Potatoes

Barb Sulser
Gooseberry Patch

Mom always made this and it became a family favorite comfort food.
You can flour and brown the pork chops before adding
to the slow cooker if you like.

1 onion, sliced, separated into
   rings and divided
8 potatoes, peeled, sliced and
   divided
16-oz. pkg. pasteurized process
   cheese spread, sliced and
   divided

6 boneless pork chops
salt and pepper to taste
10-3/4 oz. can cream of
   chicken soup

Spread a layer of onion rings in a slow cooker. Place a layer of
potatoes over onion rings, then a layer of cheese. Continue to layer
until slow cooker is two-thirds full. Sprinkle pork chops with salt
and pepper; place on top. Spread soup over top. Cover and cook for
6 to 8 hours on low setting, or 3 to 4 hours on high setting. Serves 6.

Tie up silverware and napkins with a length of cheery rick rack,
or even a pretty polka-dotted ribbon...so sweet.

Apple Butter BBQ Spareribs

Catherine Rivard
Moline, IL

Theses ribs taste amazing...my family absolutely loves them! For a change, try this same recipe using a pork or beef roast, but in place of the apple butter use apricot preserves.

4 lbs. pork spareribs
salt and pepper to taste
1 onion, quartered

16-oz. jar apple butter
18-oz. bottle barbecue sauce

Sprinkle ribs with salt and pepper. Place ribs on rimmed baking sheets. Bake at 350 degrees for 30 minutes; drain. Slice ribs into serving-size pieces and place in slow cooker. Add remaining ingredients. Cover and cook on low setting for 8 hours. Makes 4 to 6 servings.

Stack floral hat boxes, vintage tin picnic boxes or even vintage luggage... stylish storage for extra table linens or cookbooks.

Pork

Honeyed Pork BBQ

Penny Sherman
Cumming, GA

I like to shred the meat a bit and serve spooned into rolls with the carrots on the side.

16-oz. pkg. baby carrots
3-lb. boneless pork roast
1/2 c. barbecue sauce

1/4 c. honey
1/2 t. salt
1/4 t. pepper

Place pork and carrots in a slow cooker, arrange pork roast on top. Combine remaining ingredients in a small bowl; pour over pork. Cover and cook on low setting for 8 to 10 hours. Serves 6.

Pork Tenderloin

Carol Tumberger
Arlington Heights, IL

Whenever I want dinner with little prep time, either for myself or a friend, I can always rely on this simple recipe. It's always a hit and tastes delicious!

4-lb. pork loin roast
2 t. dried thyme

1/2 t. salt
1/2 t. pepper

Spray slow cooker with non-stick vegetable spray; place roast inside. Sprinkle roast with thyme, salt and pepper. Cover and cook on low setting for 7 to 8 hours. Remove; let stand for 5 minutes. Slice and serve. Makes 4 to 6 servings.

Game-Day Corn Chowder

Laura Fuller
Fort Wayne, IN

A savory chowder with a great mix of flavors. This is always simmering away in my slow cooker on football Saturday mornings so it's ready to enjoy by kick-off.

1 lb. smoked pork sausage
3 c. frozen hashbrowns with
   onions and peppers
2 carrots, peeled and chopped
15-oz. can creamed corn

10-3/4 oz. can cream of
   mushroom with roasted
   garlic soup
2 c. water

Brown sausage in a skillet over medium heat; drain and cut into bite-size pieces. Place sausage in a slow cooker; top with hashbrowns and carrots. In a medium bowl, combine corn, soup and water; mix until blended. Pour over sausage mixture. Cover and cook on low setting for 8 to 10 hours. Serves 6.

Spoon soup or chowder into a thermos and bring along to the high school football games...a scrumptious way to warm up at half-time!

Lazy-Day Soup

Kimberly Wacht
Tuba City, AZ

Sometimes I mix up the ingredients for this soup the night before, refrigerate and pop in the slow cooker in the morning. Delicious!

28-oz. pkg. frozen diced
  potatoes with onion and
  peppers
3 14-1/2 oz. cans chicken broth
16-oz. jar pasteurized process
  cheese sauce

10-3/4 oz. can cream of celery
  soup
1 to 2 c. diced cooked ham or
  Polish sausage, diced

Mix together all ingredients in slow cooker. Cover and cook on low setting for 6 to 8 hours, or on high setting for 3 hours. Serves 4 to 6.

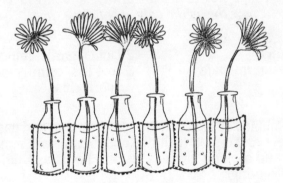

Fill empty soda pop bottles with flowers, mini American flags or pinwheels...they'll look terrific on the picnic table or porch steps.

Ginger Beer Spareribs

Katie Contario
Centreville, VA

Ginger beer gives the ribs a crisp, spicy taste.

3 lbs. center-cut pork spareribs, halved
3 12-oz. bottles ginger beer

36-oz. bottle catsup
2 c. water

Combine all ingredients in a slow cooker. Cover and cook on low setting for 8 hours. If sauce is too thin, increase slow cooker to high setting for 30 minutes. Serves 4 to 6.

Tangy Pork Ribs

JoAnn

*Thick, country-style ribs are always a family favorite...
now this is the only way I serve them.*

1/4 c. soy sauce
1/3 c. orange marmalade
3 T. catsup

2 cloves garlic, minced
3 to 4 lbs. country-style pork ribs

In a bowl, combine soy sauce, marmalade, catsup and garlic. Pour half into a slow cooker; top with ribs and drizzle with remaining sauce. Cover and cook on low setting for 6 hours, or until tender. Makes 6 to 8 servings.

Arrange several floating candles in a water-filled enamelware bowl to create a centerpiece with a soft glow.

Molly's Pork Roast

Anna McMaster
Portland, OR

My friend and I came home from a day of barn sale and flea-market shopping, to a house filled with the most delicious aroma. Our friend Molly had put this roast on before we left in the morning, knowing how good it would be to come home to dinner waiting for us.

3-lb. boneless pork roast,
   halved
8-oz. can tomato sauce

3/4 c. soy sauce
1/2 c. sugar
2 t. dry mustard

Place roast in a slow cooker. Combine remaining ingredients; pour over roast. Cover and cook on low setting for 8 to 9 hours, until a meat thermometer inserted in thickest part of roast reads 160 degrees. Remove roast; slice to serve. Makes 8 servings.

Besides the ease of letting a slow cooker do all the work, another advantage is that it uses very little electricity. On average, it costs just 21 cents to operate a slow cooker for a total of 10 hours!

Brown Sugar Ham

Melanie Lowe
Dover, DE

With only a few ingredients, you can create the most amazing flavor for this ham.

1/2 c. brown sugar, packed
1 t. dry mustard
1 t. prepared horseradish

1/4 c. cola, divided
5 to 6-lb. boneless smoked ham, halved

In a bowl, combine brown sugar, mustard, horseradish and 2 table-spoons cola; mix well. Rub over ham; place in a slow cooker. Drizzle remaining cola over ham. Cover and cook on low setting for 8 to 10 hours, or until a meat thermometer inserted in thickest part of ham reads 140 degrees. Serves 15 to 20.

Remember the old-fashioned metal ice cube dividers? Snap 'em up at the next tag sale...they make quick work of cutting homemade biscuit dough.

This & That Pork Chops

Megan Brooks
Antioch, TN

Who would have known when we tossed together what we had on hand, that these pork chops would end up so tasty?

4 pork chops	1 lemon, sliced 1/4-inch thick
1/2 t. salt	1/4 c. brown sugar, packed
1/4 t. pepper	1/4 c. catsup
1 onion, sliced 1/4-inch thick	

Place pork chops in a slow cooker; sprinkle with salt and pepper. Top with onion and lemon. Sprinkle with brown sugar; drizzle with catsup. Cover and cook on low setting for 6 hours. Makes 4 servings.

Clip-type clothespins make such handy refrigerator clips... just glue a magnet on the back and they're ideal for holding appointment cards or newspaper clippings.

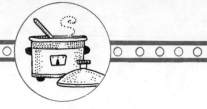

Ham & Fixin's

Kim Workman
Gastonia, NC

A recipe passed along by a friend at work, it makes a great one-pot meal that's ready when you come home from work or to take to a friend. I love slow-cooker cooking!

3 lbs. cooked ham, sliced   14-1/2 oz. can green beans
6 to 8 potatoes, peeled and diced   15-oz. can corn

Place ham in a slow cooker. Surround ham with cut potatoes, pouring green beans with juices over top. Cover and cook on low setting for 8 hours. Pour corn with juices into slow cooker 2 hours before serving. Makes 6 to 8 servings.

Slow-cooker meals make family reunion dinners so easy!
While dinner cooks, families can enjoy a game of baseball,
tag, hide & seek or just sit in the shade
catching up with one another.

Eleanor's Lentil Stew

Eleanor Paternoster
Bridgeport, CT

Jazz up this down-home stew with a swirl of pesto.

16-oz. pkg. dried lentils
4 c. water
3 c. cooked ham, diced

2 c. celery, chopped
2 c. carrots, peeled and chopped
2 10-1/2 oz. cans chicken broth

Combine all ingredients in a slow cooker. Cover and cook on low setting for 7 to 9 hours. Serves 8.

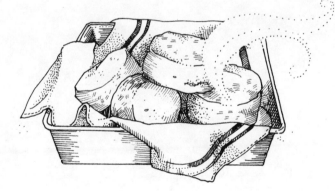

If homemade biscuits are on the menu and time has run out, don't roll dough and cut...just drop tablespoons of dough onto a lightly greased baking sheet, then bake as usual.

Pork Roast & Sauerkraut

Deirdre Foltz
Findlay, OH

I like to serve this with mashed potatoes...comfort food!

2 to 3-lb. boneless pork sirloin
   roast
32-oz. jar sauerkraut, drained
3/4 c. brown sugar, packed

1 T. caraway seed
1 Red or Golden Delicious apple,
   cored, peeled and quartered

Place pork roast in a slow cooker. In a bowl, mix together sauerkraut, brown sugar and caraway seed. Pour sauerkraut mixture over pork roast. Place quartered apples on top. Cover and cook on low setting for 8 to 10 hours, or on high setting for 4 to 5 hours. Makes 4 to 6 servings.

Keep side dishes simple...boil new potatoes just until tender, then gently toss with butter and parsley. Quick & easy!

Mom's One-Pot Dinner

Brenda Smith
Gooseberry Patch

This has always been a warm-you-to-your-toes dinner our family enjoys after a chilly day outside.

1 head cabbage, shredded
3 potatoes, peeled and cubed
1 onion, chopped
1-3/4 t. salt

1/4 t. pepper
14-1/2 oz. can chicken broth
2 lbs. Kielbasa, cut into serving-
  size pieces

In a slow cooker, combine cabbage, potatoes, onion, salt and pepper; add broth. Place Kielbasa on top. Cover and cook on low setting for 8 to 9 hours. Serves 6 to 8.

What I say is that, if a man really likes potatoes, he must be a pretty decent sort of fellow.

-A.A. Milne

Pork Chops à la Orange

Rogene Rogers
Bemidji, MN

These pork chops have the taste of a tropical luau, and they're made so easily in the slow cooker!

3 lbs. pork chops
salt and pepper
2 c. orange juice
2 11-oz. cans mandarin
   oranges, drained

8-oz. can pineapple tidbits,
   drained
cooked egg noodles

Sprinkle pork chops with salt and pepper; place in a slow cooker. Pour orange juice over pork. Cover and cook on low setting for 6 to 8 hours, or on high setting for 3 to 4 hours. About 30 minutes before serving, add oranges and pineapple; continue cooking just until warm. Serve with cooked noodles. Serves 6 to 8.

The first Sunday each August is set aside as Friendship Day...
tote a slow-cooker dinner to a friend or neighbor for
a most welcome surprise.

Sweet & Tangy Pork Roast

Carol Lytle
Columbus, OH

*I like to put this roast in the slow cooker early on New Year's Day...
we enjoy the parades and football games, then settle in that
evening for a really great dinner.*

2-1/2 lb. boneless pork
  shoulder roast
1 c. sweetened, dried
  cranberries
1/2 c. chicken broth

1/2 c. cranberry juice cocktail,
  divided
1/2 t. salt
1/8 t. pepper
2 T. cornstarch

Place roast in a slow cooker. Combine cranberries, broth, 1/4 cup
juice, salt and pepper in a small bowl; pour over roast. Cover and
cook on low setting for 7 to 9 hours. Remove roast; cover with
aluminum foil to keep warm. Pour juices from slow cooker into
a medium saucepan. Combine remaining juice with cornstarch in a
small bowl; mix well. Stir into juices in saucepan; cook and stir over
medium heat until thickened and bubbly, about 3 minutes. Serve
with roast. Makes 6 servings.

Use colorful oilcloth
to dress up buffet
tables...so much
nicer than plastic
tablecloths and it
simply wipes clean.

Saucy Ribs

Zoe Bennett
Columbia, SC

Better make plenty...these will disappear quickly!

1 t. dry mustard	3 lbs. baby back pork ribs,
1/2 t. allspice	sliced into 4-inch pieces
1 t. salt	1/2 c. water
1 t. pepper	1-1/2 c. barbecue sauce

Combine all seasonings in a small bowl; rub onto ribs. Place in a slow cooker and pour water over top. Cover and cook on low setting for 8 to 9 hours, until ribs are tender when pierced with a fork. Remove ribs from slow cooker; discard cooking liquid. Replace ribs in slow cooker and add barbecue sauce. Cover and cook on low setting for one additional hour. Makes 6 servings.

Welcome family & friends with greetings written on helium-filled balloons! Permanent markers make it easy to decorate balloons in so many ways.

What-If Ham

Tonya Sheppard
Galveston, TX

Without any cola on hand for our usual cola ham recipe, we tried lemon-lime soda and said "What if we use this instead?" I'm so glad we did...what a hit it was!

3 to 4-lb. fully-cooked ham
12-oz. can lemon-lime soda
1/4 c. honey

1/2 t. dry mustard
1/2 t. ground cloves
1/4 t. cinnamon

Place ham in a slow cooker; add soda. Cover and cook on low setting for 6 to 8 hours, or on high setting for 3 to 4 hours. About 30 minutes before serving, combine 3 tablespoons juices from slow cooker with honey, mustard and spices. Mix well and spread over ham. Cover and continue cooking on low setting for 30 minutes. Let stand for 15 minutes before slicing. Makes 12 to 16 servings.

For recipes with fresh-picked flavor year 'round, keep a pot of chives, parsley or sage growing on the windowsill.

Easy-Does-It Ribs

Jackie Lowe
Maysville, KY

The flavor of barbecue sauce combined with Catalina dressing makes a really tasty sauce, and with 3 ingredients, it's so easy to prepare.

3-1/2 to 4 lbs. country-style
  pork ribs

1 c. barbecue sauce
1 c. Catalina salad dressing

Spray a slow cooker with non-stick vegetable spray. Place ribs in slow cooker. Mix together barbecue sauce and salad dressing; pour over ribs. Cover and cook on low setting for 8 hours. Makes 6 to 8 servings.

Country-Style Ribs

Nichole Martelli
Santa Fe, TX

*This has become my husband's favorite way to prepare ribs...
he likes this better than ribs cooked on the grill!*

2 lbs. boneless country-style
  pork ribs, cut into serving-
  size pieces
1 onion, sliced

3 cloves garlic, minced
2/3 c. barbecue sauce
1/3 c. apple jelly

Place ribs, onion and garlic in a slow cooker that has been sprayed with non-stick vegetable spray. Cover and cook on low setting for 8 to 10 hours. Drain and discard cooking liquid. In a small bowl, combine barbecue sauce and jelly; spread evenly over ribs. Cover and cook on high setting for an additional 25 minutes, or until ribs are glazed. Serves 4 to 6.

Golden Potatoes & Ham

Marilyn Morel
Keene, NH

My children and husband love this dish. I serve it with sliced peaches
and warm French bread...comfort food at its best.

6 c. potatoes, peeled and sliced
2-1/2 c. cooked ham, cubed
1-1/2 c. shredded Cheddar
  cheese

10-3/4 oz. can cream of
  mushroom soup
1/2 c. evaporated milk

In a slow cooker, layer one-third each of potatoes, ham and cheese.
Repeat layers 2 more times. Combine soup and milk and blend until
smooth; pour over potato mixture. Cover and cook on low setting for
7 to 8 hours. Makes 4 to 6 servings.

So simple...dress up the stems of water glasses with
a few sprigs of fresh herbs.

Harvest Pork Roast

Darrell Lawry
Kissimmee, FL

I like to put this roast on early in the morning when we know we'll be gone all day.

2 to 3-lb. boneless pork loin
   roast
14-1/2 oz. can chicken broth
1 c. unsweetened apple juice

1/2 c. Dijon mustard
6 T. cold water
6 T. cornstarch

Place roast in a slow cooker. Combine broth, apple juice and mustard; pour over roast. Cover and cook on low setting for 4 to 5 hours, or until a meat thermometer inserted in thickest part of roast reads 160 degrees. Remove roast and keep warm. For gravy, skim fat and strain cooking liquids into a small saucepan. Combine water and cornstarch until smooth; gradually stir into juices. Bring to a boil over medium-high heat; cook and stir for 2 minutes, or until thickened. Serve with sliced pork. Makes 8 servings.

Mango Chutney Ham

Marlene Darnell
Newport Beach, CA

A truly flavorful ham.

3-lb. fully-cooked ham
2 6-oz. jars mango chutney
1 onion, chopped

1 T. balsamic vinegar
1/4 t. pepper

Place ham in slow cooker. Mix remaining ingredients in a medium bowl; pour over ham. Cover and cook on low setting for 6 to 8 hours. Serve juices over sliced ham. Makes 6 to 8 servings.

Sunday Pork Roast Dinner

Diana Chaney
Olathe, KS

There's nothing like coming home from Sunday meetings to find a dinner that's ready to enjoy.

2 apples, cored, peeled and
   chopped
1 onion, chopped
3 T. honey mustard
2-lb. boneless pork roast

1/4 t. salt
1/4 t. pepper
2 T. cold water
1 T. cornstarch

Combine apples and onion in a slow cooker. Spread mustard over pork roast; sprinkle with salt and pepper. Place roast on top of apple mixture. Cover and cook on low setting for 7 to 8 hours. Remove roast and cover with aluminum foil to keep warm. Whisk together water and cornstarch in a medium saucepan. Add cooking liquid, apples and onion; cook over medium heat until mixture boils and thickens, stirring frequently. Serve roast with sauce. Makes 8 servings.

In the sweetness of friendship, let there be laughter
and sharing of pleasures.
-Kahlil Gibran

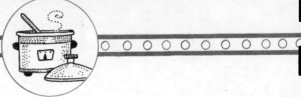

Slow-Cooker Ribs

Dianna Hamilton
Beaverton, OR

This is a quick recipe for spareribs in the slow cooker.
The result? Very, very tender ribs.

8 boneless pork spareribs
1 onion, thinly sliced and
   separated into rings

8-oz. bottle barbecue sauce

Place spareribs in a slow cooker; top with onion. Pour barbecue sauce over ribs and onion. Cover and cook on low setting for 8 to 9 hours. Makes 3 to 4 servings.

Copies of handwritten recipe cards make the sweetest cookbook covers. Simply attach copies with spray adhesive, then smooth the edges.

Sandwiches

Jenny's BBQ Beef Sandwiches

Jenny Bishoff
Swanton, MD

These are especially good on split, toasted potato buns.

2 lbs. stew beef, cubed
18-oz. bottle barbecue sauce

12-oz. can cola
6 to 8 sandwich buns, split

Mix together all ingredients except buns in slow cooker. Cover and cook on low setting for 6 to 8 hours. Serve on buns. Makes 6 to 8 sandwiches.

Virginia-Style Beef Sandwiches

Ursula Juarez-Wall
Dumfries, VA

Add a side of coleslaw or potato salad, and you have
the makings for a picnic!

2-1/2 to 3-lb. beef round or
   shoulder roast
1 c. catsup
12-oz. can beer or non-alcoholic
   beer

1-1/2 oz. pkg. onion soup mix
8 hamburger buns, split
Garnish: bottled barbecue sauce

Place roast in slow cooker; set aside. Mix together catsup, beer and soup mix in a bowl; pour over roast. Cover and cook on low setting for 4 to 4-1/2 hours. Shred roast with 2 forks. Spoon shredded beef onto buns and serve topped with barbecue sauce. Makes 8 sandwiches.

National Sandwich Day is November 3rd...celebrate and
serve up a favorite sandwich!

Southern BBQ

Cyndi Little
Whitsett, NC

Serve this either as a main dish with sides or on hamburger buns with slaw for a truly great North Carolina-style meal.

1 c. cider vinegar
2 T. sugar
1 T. salt
3 to 4-lb. pork loin roast

1 T. Worcestershire sauce
1/2 c. catsup
Optional: hot sauce to taste
6 to 8 sandwich buns, split

Mix together vinegar, sugar and salt. Pour over roast in a slow cooker. Cover and cook on low setting for 10 to 12 hours, until meat pulls from bones. Remove and cool; pull apart and shred. Mix 6 to 8 tablespoons of cooking liquid with Worcestershire sauce and catsup. Pour over meat and add hot sauce to taste, if desired; mix well. Spoon shredded meat and sauce onto buns. Makes 6 to 8 sandwiches.

Try something new...onion buns topped with shredded chicken or saucy BBQ taste great!

Chicken-Stuffing Sandwiches

Amber Beckman
Garden City, MI

Serving 20 to 25, you'll find this recipe ideal for family reunions, church suppers or feeding the team after a big game.

50-oz. can chicken
6-oz. pkg. chicken-flavored
  stuffing mix
10-3/4 oz. can cream of chicken
  soup

10-1/2 oz. can chicken broth
20 to 25 sandwich buns, split

Combine chicken with juice and remaining ingredients except buns in a slow cooker. Cover and cook on low setting for 4 hours, or on high setting for 2 hours. Spoon onto sandwich buns. Makes 20 to 25 sandwiches.

California Chicken Tacos

Dawn Morgan
Glendora, CA

This recipe is great for those days when you know the evening will be hectic!

1 lb. boneless, skinless chicken
  breasts
1-1/4 oz. pkg. taco seasoning
  mix
16-oz. jar favorite salsa

8 to 10 corn taco shells
Garnish: shredded lettuce,
  diced tomatoes, sour cream,
  shredded Cheddar cheese

Combine all ingredients except taco shells and garnish. Cover and cook on low setting for 6 to 8 hours, or on high setting for 4 hours. Shred chicken and spoon into taco shells; garnish as desired. Makes 8 to 10 tacos.

Try sprinkling chicken with a bit of fajita seasoning
while cooking. What a flavor boost!

Pork Sandwich Spread

Janie Reed
Gooseberry Patch

This simple recipe helped my mom feed our large family. It was always a welcome meal on a cold winter day.

2 to 3-lb. pork roast
1/4 t. dried basil
1/4 t. dried oregano
salt and pepper to taste

3 eggs
1 sleeve round buttery crackers
20 sandwich buns, split

Place roast in a slow cooker; sprinkle with seasonings. Cover and cook on high setting for 2 to 3 hours, until fork-tender. Remove roast; cool. Reserve 1/2 cup cooking liquid. Grind meat with a meat grinder; add eggs and crushed crackers. Add reserved liquid and enough water to obtain consistency of thick soup. Return meat mixture to slow cooker and cook on low setting for an additional 2 hours. Spoon onto warm buns. Makes 20 sandwiches.

Simple Shredded Pork Tacos

Christine Horjus
Hebron, IN

I like to serve my tacos with shredded cheese, lettuce, chopped tomatoes and sour cream.

2-lb. boneless pork loin roast
1 c. salsa
4-oz. can chopped green chiles
1/2 t. garlic salt

1/2 t. pepper
Optional: 7-1/2 oz. bottle mild
   taco sauce
8 10-inch flour tortillas, warmed

Combine all ingredients in a slow cooker except taco sauce and tortillas. Cover and cook on low setting for about 8 hours; drain juices. Shred pork and return to slow cooker. If desired, add taco sauce; heat through. Serve on tortillas. Makes 6 to 8 tacos.

Italian Roast Beef Sandwiches

Pamela Meddaugh
Chippewa Falls, WI

I use this recipe often...it gets so many compliments.

4-lb. beef chuck roast, halved	1 t. pepper
10-1/2 oz. can French onion	1 t. garlic powder
soup	1 t. dried oregano
2/3 c. beer or non-alcoholic beer	6 to 8 sandwich buns, split
1 t. salt	and toasted

Place roast in a slow cooker. Combine remaining ingredients except buns in a bowl; pour over roast. Cover and cook on low setting for 7 hours. Slice roast thinly and serve on toasted buns. Makes 6 to 8 sandwiches.

French Dip Au Jus

Sharon Mull
McKinney, TX

This is a recipe my mother has passed on to me, and it's a favorite in my family now. Oh my! How wonderful the kitchen smells when I walk in the door after it's been simmering all day.

3 to 4-lb. beef rump roast	1-1/2 oz. pkg. onion soup mix
1 c. soy sauce	6 to 8 hoagie buns, split

Place roast in a slow cooker; pour soy sauce over top. Sprinkle soup mix over roast; fill slow cooker with enough water to cover roast. Cover and cook on low setting for 10 to 12 hours. Slice or shred meat; serve on rolls. Pour juices from slow cooker into small bowls for dipping. Makes 6 to 8 sandwiches.

Louisiana Sausage Sandwiches
Dana Cunningham
Lafayette, LA

After working the county fair one year with a friend, I learned how to make these sandwiches like a pro!

19.76-oz. pkg. Italian pork
  sausage links
1 green pepper, sliced into
  bite-size pieces
1 onion, sliced into bite-size
  pieces

8-oz. can tomato sauce
1/8 t. pepper
6 hoagie rolls, split

In a large skillet, brown sausage links over medium heat. Cut into 1/2-inch slices; place in a slow cooker. Stir in remaining ingredients except rolls. Cover and cook on low setting for 8 hours. Spoon onto rolls with a slotted spoon. Makes 6 sandwiches.

Place onions in the freezer for just 5 minutes before slicing them...no more tears!

All-American Cheeseburgers

Claire Bertram
Lexington, KY

Who needs a grill? These are scrumptious!

1 lb. ground beef, browned and
   drained
3 T. catsup
2 t. mustard

2 c. pasteurized process cheese
   spread, cubed
10 hamburger buns, split

Place ground beef in a slow cooker; add catsup and mustard, mixing well. Top with cubed cheese. Cover and cook on low setting for 3 to 4 hours. Stir beef mixture gently; spoon onto buns. Makes 10 sandwiches.

Tote the slow cooker to a backyard campout! Bring flashlights, catch lots of fireflies, sing songs, make shadow puppets and snuggle up in sleeping bags...what wonderful memories you'll make.

Tex-Mex Chili Dogs

Stacie Mickley
Gooseberry Patch

With green chiles and corn chips in this recipe, regular chili dogs
are a thing of the past at our home.

1-lb. pkg. hot dogs
2 15-oz. cans chili without
  beans
10-3/4 oz. can Cheddar cheese
  soup

4-oz. can chopped green chiles
10 hot dog buns, split
Garnish: chopped onion,
  crushed corn chips, shredded
  Cheddar cheese

Place hot dogs in a slow cooker. In a large bowl, combine chili, soup
and green chiles; pour over hot dogs. Cover and cook on low setting
for 4 to 5 hours. Serve hot dogs in buns; top with chili mixture and
garnish as desired. Makes 10 sandwiches.

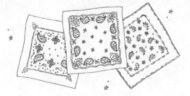

Taco Joes

Sherry, Cress
Salem, IN

Try garnishing with a little peach or pineapple salsa...really good!

3 lbs. ground beef, browned and
  drained
16-oz. can refried beans
10-oz. can enchilada sauce
1-1/4 oz. pkg. taco seasoning
  mix

16-oz. jar salsa
25 hot dog buns, split
Garnish: shredded Cheddar
  cheese, shredded lettuce,
  chopped tomatoes,
  sour cream

Place ground beef in a slow cooker. Stir in beans, enchilada sauce,
taco seasoning and salsa. Cover and cook on low setting for 4 to
6 hours. To serve, fill each bun with 1/3 cup beef mixture and
garnish as desired. Makes 25 sandwiches.

A Dilly of a Sandwich

Marian Buckley
Fontana, CA

Everyone will ask for seconds on these dilly beef sandwiches...they're packed with flavor.

3 to 4-lb. boneless beef chuck
   roast, halved
16-oz. jar whole dill pickles

1/2 c. chili sauce
2 cloves garlic, minced
10 to 12 hamburger buns, split

Place roast in a slow cooker; add pickles with juice, chili sauce and garlic. Cover and cook on low setting for 8 to 9 hours, until beef is tender. Remove and discard pickles. Reserve cooking liquid in slow cooker. Remove roast and let stand until cool enough to handle; shred with 2 forks. Return to slow cooker and heat through. With a slotted spoon, fill each bun with about 1/2 cup meat mixture. Makes 10 to 12 sandwiches.

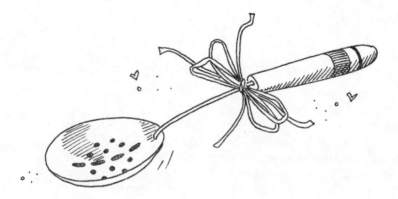

French Dip Sandwiches

Patricia Rodgers
Brookshire, TX

This is my own original recipe, which I submitted to my high school alumni cookbook about 20 years ago. When the cookbook was reviewed by the Omaha World Herald, I was thrilled to find my recipe was featured in the newspaper!

3 to 4-lb. beef chuck roast
1-1/4 oz. pkg. buttermilk ranch
   salad dressing mix

14-1/2 oz. can beef broth
1 loaf French bread, sliced

Place roast in a slow cooker. Cover and cook on low setting for 6 to 8 hours. Remove from slow cooker; shred with 2 forks. Return to slow cooker; sprinkle with dressing mix. Add broth and cook on low setting for an additional 2 hours. Serve on French bread with a small bowl of juices from slow cooker for dipping. Makes 6 to 8 sandwiches.

French Dip Sandwiches are so deliciously juicy! To keep that juice from dripping, wrap individual servings in aluminum foil, then peel back as they're eaten.

Lisa's Shredded Beef Sandwiches

*Lisa Nehring
Parker, SD*

*This beef is also great served with noodles or used for
burritos or enchiladas.*

2 2 to 3-lb. beef top round
   roasts
1.05-oz. pkg. Italian salad
   dressing mix

1.35-oz. pkg. onion soup mix
15-oz. can tomatoes with chiles
1/2 c. water
10 to 12 sandwich buns, split

Rub roasts with dressing mix and soup mix. Place in a slow cooker.
Cover and cook on low setting for 5 to 6 hours. Remove meat and
shred. Refrigerate juices until cold, skim fat off the top and discard.
Return meat to slow cooker with juices. Cover and cook on high
setting until heated through. Spoon meat onto buns. Makes 10 to
12 sandwiches.

It's easy to shake up sandwiches at dinnertime...just offer a
variety of breads to choose from. Focaccia, rye, pumpernickle,
pita bread and raisin bread all make terrifically tasty sandwiches!

Zesty Italian Beef

Jennifer Maxey
Mount Vernon, IL

The beef will shred so easily that sandwiches are a breeze to make.

3-lb. beef chuck roast, quartered
1 to 2 T. oil
2-oz. pkg. zesty Italian salad
 dressing mix
12-oz. can beer or non-alcoholic
 beer

1 onion, chopped
6 to 7 pepperoncini peppers,
 chopped
6 to 8 sandwich buns, split

Brown roast in oil in a skillet over medium heat; place into a slow cooker. Sprinkle with dressing mix; pour beer over top. Add onion and peppers. Cook on high setting heat for 5 to 6 hours, until meat shreds easily with a fork. Spoon onto sandwich buns. Makes 6 to 8 sandwiches.

Some recipes only call for half an onion, so save prep time on a future recipe...just chop and freeze the other half right away.

Lemon-Garlic Chicken Tacos

Marion Sundberg
Ramona, CA

This recipe is excellent in tacos, tostadas, enchiladas or any other recipe that calls for shredded chicken. My family really likes the lemon taste so I use a lot of lemon juice. For a milder taste, use chicken broth.

6 boneless, skinless chicken
   breasts
1 to 1-1/2 c. lemon juice or
   chicken broth
5 to 6 cloves garlic

salt and pepper to taste
12 corn taco shells
Garnish: shredded lettuce,
   chopped tomatoes, shredded
   Cheddar cheese

Place chicken in a slow cooker. Cover and cook on low setting for 8 hours; drain. Shred chicken and return to slow cooker; add lemon juice to cover, garlic, salt and pepper. Cover and cook on low setting for an additional 4 to 5 hours. Serve in taco shells and garnish as desired. Makes 12 sandwiches.

Use the last few minutes Lemon-Garlic Chicken Tacos are cooking to whip up a speedy black bean salad. Combine one cup drained and rinsed black beans, 1/2 cup frozen corn, 1/2 cup salsa and 1/4 teaspoon cumin or chili powder; stir well.

Carolina Chicken Pitas

Sharon Tillman
Hampton, VA

The way we enjoy pitas down south!

1 onion, chopped
1 lb. boneless, skinless chicken
  thighs
1 t. lemon-pepper seasoning

1/2 t. dried oregano
1/2 c. plain yogurt
4 pita bread rounds, halved
  and split

Combine all ingredients except yogurt and pitas in a slow cooker; mix well. Cover and cook on low setting for 6 to 8 hours. Just before serving, remove chicken from slow cooker and shred with 2 forks. Return shredded chicken back to slow cooker; stir in yogurt. Spoon into pita bread. Makes 4 sandwiches.

Serve this Greek version of bruschetta alongside Carolina Chicken Pitas. Grill thick slices of sourdough bread until golden, then brush with olive oil, spread with tomatoes to cover bread, sprinkle to taste with crumbled feta and dried oregano.

Italian Sausage Subs

Cheri Maxwell
Gulf Breeze, FL

*A classic sub sandwich...the kind you get in a
mom & pop pizza shop!*

19.76-oz. pkg. Italian pork
   sausage links
1 green pepper, sliced
1 onion, sliced

26-oz. jar spaghetti sauce
5 sub buns, split
Garnish: 5 slices provolone
   cheese

In a non-stick skillet over medium heat, cook sausage until brown.
Place in a slow cooker; add pepper and onion. Top with spaghetti
sauce. Cover and cook on low setting for 4 to 6 hours. Place sausages
in buns; top with sauce mixture from slow cooker and cheese. Makes
5 sandwiches.

With dinner practically preparing itself in the slow cooker,
now's the perfect time to catch up on that book you've
been meaning to finish. Make a handy bookmark in
no time at all...choose a 12-inch length of ribbon
and stitch a pompom at each end!

Tangy Teriyaki Sandwiches

Kelly Alderson
Erie, PA

What a combination of flavors...what a winner!

1-1/2 lbs. skinless turkey thighs
1/2 c. teriyaki baste and
  glaze sauce
3 T. orange marmalade
1/4 t. pepper
4 hoagie buns, split

Combine all ingredients except buns in a slow cooker; cover and cook on low setting for 9 to 10 hours. Remove turkey and shred meat, discarding bones; return to slow cooker. Cover and cook on high setting for 10 to 15 minutes, until sauce is thickened. Serve on hoagie buns. Makes 4 sandwiches.

Cool down with the flavor of real, homemade ice cream. Buy an old-fashioned ice cream maker...the kind with a crank handle! The kids will love taking turns cranking, and Grandma will have some sweet stories to share about how she did the very same thing at their age.

Saucy Meatball Hoagies

Dana Thompson
Gooseberry Patch

Better get the lap-size napkins out for this feast.

40 frozen meatballs, thawed
26-oz. jar pasta sauce
1 onion, chopped

6 hoagie buns, split and toasted
6 slices Muenster cheese

Combine meatballs, pasta sauce and onion in a slow cooker. Cover and cook on low setting for 4 to 6 hours. Place meatballs in toasted hoagie buns and top with cheese. Broil to melt cheese, if desired. Makes 6 sandwiches.

Try spooning any favorite sandwich filling into a pita pocket...
less mess!

Brisket Roll Sandwiches

Kimberley O'Rourke
Irving, TX

A genuine southern treat...Texas-style!

3 to 4-lb. boneless beef brisket
1/2 c. mustard
1/2 c. Dijon mustard

1.35-oz. pkg. onion soup mix
6 to 8 potato rolls, split

Place brisket in a slow cooker that has been sprayed with non-stick vegetable spray. In a small bowl, mix together mustards; brush over brisket. Sprinkle soup mix over brisket. Cover and cook on low setting for 7 to 8 hours. Slice brisket and serve on potato rolls. Makes 6 to 8 sandwiches.

Wherever you go, no matter what the weather,
always bring your own sunshine.
-Anthony J. D'Angelo

Pulled Pork Sandwiches

Alice Schnelle
Oak Lawn, IL

A big scoop of coleslaw makes this a complete meal.

4-lb. pork shoulder roast
2 onions, sliced into rings
6 whole cloves
salt and pepper to taste
2 c. water

18-oz. bottle honey barbecue
  sauce
8 to 12 hard rolls, split
Garnish: coleslaw

Combine all ingredients except rolls and coleslaw in a slow cooker.
Cover and cook on low setting for 10 hours, or on high setting for
5 hours. Remove roast and shred meat, discarding any cooking liquid.
Return pork to slow cooker; add sauce to taste. Cover and cook on high
setting for one to 2 hours, until heated through, stirring occasionally.
Serve on rolls with a side of coleslaw. Makes 8 to 12 sandwiches.

Nifty 1950's juice glasses are filled with whimsy...
snap 'em up at flea markets, tuck in tea lights
and enjoy their fun vintage designs.

Midwest Chicken Sandwiches

Kathleen Felton
Fairfax, IA

*This is one of my most-requested potluck recipes. I always bring
copies of the recipe with me and when I leave I bring home
an empty slow cooker.*

4 skinless chicken thighs
4 skinless chicken breasts
1/4 t. garlic salt
1.35-oz. pkg. onion soup mix

1/4 c. Italian salad dressing
1/4 c. water
12 hamburger buns, split

Place chicken in a slow cooker; sprinkle with garlic salt and soup
mix. Add remaining ingredients. Cover and cook on low setting for
7 to 8 hours. Remove chicken; cool slightly. Shred chicken; discard
bones. Return shredded chicken to slow cooker to keep warm. Spoon
onto buns. Makes 12 sandwiches.

Try freezing bright berries inside ice cubes and dropping
them into punch...mint leaves are pretty too!

Savory Pork Carnitas

Lisa Wagner
Delaware, OH

Try this recipe the next time you're craving tacos or burritos. You can also enjoy it as a main dish topped with all the garnishes.

3 to 4-lb. Boston butt pork roast
1-1/4 oz. pkg. taco seasoning
   mix
3 cloves garlic, sliced
1 onion, quartered
4-oz. can green chiles, drained
3/4 to 1 c. water

6 to 8 flour tortillas
Garnish: shredded lettuce,
   chopped tomatoes, sliced
   avocado, sour cream, lime
   wedges, sliced green onions,
   fresh cilantro sprigs

Combine pork, taco seasoning, garlic, onion and chiles in a slow cooker. Add water, using the full amount if pork is closer to 4 pounds; stir to combine. Cover and cook for 10 hours on low setting, or 6 hours on high setting, until tender enough to shred. Spoon shredded pork down center of tortillas and serve with desired garnishes. Makes 8 servings.

Dinnertime with a Mexican feel...give everyone a sombrero and a pair of maracas as they get seated!

Shredded Beef Tacos

Jennifer Gregory
Columbia City, IN

The shredded beef makes these tacos a meal in themselves. Of course,
a side of Mexican rice or refried beans is always welcome.

3-lb. beef chuck roast
2 onions, sliced
2 c. water
2 1-1/4 oz. pkgs. taco
   seasoning mix
2 16-oz. jars taco sauce

2 4-oz. cans diced green chilies
24 corn taco shells
Garnish: shredded lettuce,
   chopped tomato, shredded
   Cheddar cheese, sour cream

Place beef and onions in a slow cooker. Combine water and seasoning
mix in a small bowl; pour over beef and onions. Cover and cook on
low setting for 6 to 8 hours. Remove meat; shred with 2 forks. Place
beef in a large bowl; stir in taco sauce and chiles. Fill warmed taco
shells with beef mixture. Top with lettuce, tomato, cheese and sour
cream. Makes 12 servings, 2 tacos each.

When the summertime garden is bursting with tomatoes, peppers
and onions, make homemade salsa...it's a snap. Combine as
much as you like of chopped tomatoes, onions and jalapeño
peppers...add some fresh cilantro, salt and lime juice. You can't
go wrong...adjust the amounts to suit your own taste!

Mom's Shredded BBQ

Lori Drew
Ely, NV

This works well with a pork roast too!

2 lbs. beef roast, cubed
1 onion, coarsely chopped
1 green or red pepper, coarsely
   chopped
18-oz. bottle favorite barbecue
   sauce

1/4 to 1/2 c. water
4 to 6 hard rolls or hamburger
   buns, split
Garnish: sliced red onion,
   dill pickles

Place beef in a slow cooker; top with vegetables, barbecue sauce and
water. Cover and cook on low setting for 6 to 8 hours, until meat
shreds easily. Using 2 forks, shred meat and return to slow cooker
to keep warm. Serve on rolls or buns, topped with slices of red onion
and dill pickles. Makes 4 to 6 sandwiches.

Pork BBQ Sandwiches

Debbie Roberts
Columbus, IN

A can't-be-beat favorite when served with coleslaw and chips.

12 boneless pork chops,
   1/2-inch thick
1/2 c. water
1/2 t. salt
1/4 t. pepper
1/4 t. cayenne pepper

1/4 t. onion powder
1/4 t. garlic powder
18-oz. bottle hickory or
   honey barbecue sauce
8 kaiser rolls, split

Layer pork chops in a slow cooker; add water. Sprinkle with
seasonings. Cover and cook on high setting for one hour. Reduce
heat to low setting and cook for an additional 6 to 8 hours; drain.
Chop pork into bite-size pieces. Add barbecue sauce; cover and cook
on low setting until heated through, about 30 minutes. Pile pork on
rolls to serve. Makes 8 sandwiches.

Sides & Veggies

Creamy Dijon Potatoes

Donna Fisher
Gooseberry Patch

*If you choose to add a dash of cayenne, it really spices up
these yummy potatoes.*

6 potatoes, peeled and sliced
10-3/4 oz. can cream of chicken
  soup
3 T. Dijon mustard

1 onion, sliced
1 green pepper, sliced
Optional: 1 t. cayenne pepper

Place potatoes in slow cooker. Combine soup and mustard; spread
over potatoes. Top with onion and green pepper. Sprinkle with
cayenne pepper, if desired. Cover and cook on low setting for
6 to 8 hours. Serves 4.

Dinnertime is a terrific way to slow down and catch up
with family. Talk about what everybody did that day,
the plans for the week, and even look ahead to the weekend.

Parsley Buttered Potatoes

Kendall Hale
Lynn, MA

Butter, chives and a dash of lemon juice jump-start
a super-easy, super-tasting recipe.

1-1/2 lbs. new redskin potatoes
1/4 c. water
1/4 c. butter, melted
1 T. lemon juice

3 T. fresh parsley, minced
1 T. fresh chives, snipped
salt and pepper to taste

If desired, pare a strip around the middle of each potato. Place potatoes and water in a slow cooker. Cover and cook on high setting for 2-1/2 to 3 hours, until tender; drain. In a small bowl, combine butter, lemon juice, parsley and chives. Pour over potatoes; toss to coat. Sprinkle with salt and pepper. Serves 6.

When garnishing a dish, instead of using parsley, use your favorite chopped fresh herb or quartered cherry tomatoes.

Easy Family-Style Corn

Katie Dick
Olathe, KS

This is a favorite side to any meal!

2 12-oz pkgs. frozen corn
8-oz. pkg. cream cheese, cubed
1/4 c. butter, cubed

2 T. sugar
1 t. salt
1/2 t. pepper

Spray a slow cooker with non-stick vegetable spray. Add all ingredients; stir to mix. Cover and cook on low setting for 4 hours, stirring halfway through. Makes 8 to 10 servings.

Spiff up mashed potatoes with very little effort...toss in snipped chives, shredded cheese, minced garlic or bacon bits.

Barbecue Molasses Beans

Connie Hilty
Pearland, TX

These beans taste so good, nobody will know you didn't spend all day in the kitchen.

16-oz. pkg. dried pinto beans
3 c. water
1 onion, chopped

18-oz. bottle barbecue sauce
1/4 c. molasses
1/4 t. pepper

Combine all ingredients in a slow cooker; mix well. Cover and cook on low setting for 8 to 9 hours. Serves 6 to 8.

Macaroni & Cheese

Vicki Lanzendorf
Madison, WI

This is great to make on a Saturday when we have to be at the ballpark all afternoon. To make a heartier version, I sometimes add cooked and diced ham or chicken, celery and onion. This recipe is also the only thing I'm "allowed" to bring to our office potlucks...everyone there loves it too.

1/2 c. butter
1/2 c. all-purpose flour
2 t. salt
4 c. milk
16-oz. pkg. pasteurized process cheese spread, cubed

16-oz. pkg. elbow macaroni, cooked
paprika to taste

Melt butter in a saucepan over medium heat; stir in flour and salt. Gradually add milk and stir until thickened. Add cheese, stirring until melted. Combine macaroni and cheese sauce in a slow cooker; sprinkle with paprika. Cover and cook on low setting for 4 hours. Makes 12 to 16 servings.

Parsnips with a Twist

Robin Hill
Rochester, NY

Only 3 ingredients, but together they make this dish tasty and unique.

2 T. olive oil
1 T. soy sauce

1 lb. parsnips, peeled and sliced
1/2-inch thick

Mix together oil and soy sauce; add to a slow cooker. Stir in parsnips until evenly coated. Cover and cook on high setting until tender, about 3 to 4 hours. Makes 4 to 6 servings.

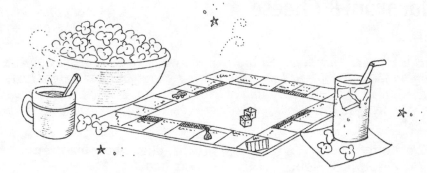

Start the week off right...make Monday night family night!
Play games, read stories...with dinner cooking away in
the slow cooker, there's plenty of time for fun!

Mom's Honey-Glazed Carrots

Regina Vining
Warwick, RI

It's the addition of honey that makes these carrots so popular.
They're sure to be another one of your favorite recipes.

2-lb. pkg. baby carrots
1-1/2 c. water
1/4 c. honey

2 T. butter, softened
1/4 t. salt
1/8 t. pepper

Combine carrots and water in a slow cooker. Cover and cook on low setting for 6 to 8 hours. Drain carrots and return to slow cooker. Stir in honey, butter, salt and pepper; mix well. Cover and cook on low setting for an additional 30 minutes, until glazed. Makes 6 to 8 servings.

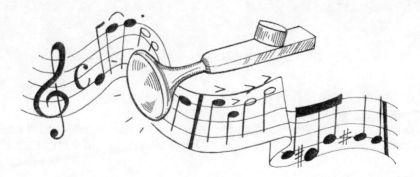

Laughter is the best dinnertime music.

–Carleton Kendrick

Wisconsin Bacon-Potato Soup

Debbie Hundley
Barron, WI

Wisconsin winters can be very cold, lasting from November sometimes into March! You'll find keeping a slow cooker filled with this soup on hand is the best for a warming winter supper, or any time you crave a comforting, creamy soup.

5 lbs. potatoes, peeled and
   chopped
1/2 lb. bacon, crisply cooked
   and crumbled
1 onion, chopped

8-oz. container sour cream
3 14-1/2 oz. cans chicken broth
10-3/4 oz. cream of chicken
   soup

Combine all ingredients in a slow cooker. Cover and cook on low setting for 8 to 10 hours, or on high setting for 4 to 5 hours. Serves 6 to 8.

Easy Clam Chowder

Debbie Cassar
Rockford, MI

This is so easy and it tastes like you cooked over a stove all day!

3 10-3/4 oz. cans cream of
   potato soup
2 10-3/4 oz. cans New England
   clam chowder

1/2 c. butter, diced
1 pt. half-and-half
2 6-1/2 oz. cans chopped clams
1/3 c. sherry or chicken broth

Combine first 4 ingredients in slow cooker; mix well. Drain clam juice into slow cooker; set clams aside. Cover and cook on low setting for 2 to 4 hours. During last 45 minutes of cooking, stir in clams and sherry or broth. Makes 4 to 6 servings.

Cheesy Broccoli Soup

Robyn Fiedler
Buckley, WA

Super easy to prepare, this soup is perfect with a sandwich,
or even makes a meal by itself.

2 10-3/4 oz. cans cream of
  celery soup
16-oz. pkg. frozen chopped
  broccoli

16-oz. jar pasteurized process
  cheese sauce
2 cubes chicken bouillon
1 pt. half-and-half

Blend all ingredients in a slow cooker. Cover and cook on low setting
for 4 to 6 hours. Serves 6.

Soup is so nice when shared. Thank a friend with a basket
of warm rolls and a pot of steaming homemade soup.
What a welcome surprise on a brisk day!

Tina's Baked Beans

Tina Wallace
Calverton, NY

A potluck-perfect dish!

1 lb. bacon, cut into 1-inch
  pieces and crisply cooked
2 28-oz. cans baked beans

1-1/2 c. brown sugar, packed
1/4 c. molasses

Combine all ingredients in a slow cooker; mix well. Cover and cook on high setting for 5 hours. Reduce heat to low setting; continue cooking an additional 5 hours. Makes 8 to 10 servings.

Serve up baked beans cowboy style...enjoy them with a dinner 'round a campfire! Roast hot dogs, grill corn on the cob, flame roast potatoes and top dinner off with warm biscuits and honey.

Homestyle Green Beans

Eva Jo Hoyle
Mexico, MO

Really flavorful green beans...ideal alongside any family dinner.

3 14-1/2 oz. cans green beans,
  drained
6 slices bacon, crisply cooked
  and crumbled

1/2 c. onion, chopped
1 c. catsup
1 c. brown sugar, packed

Mix all ingredients together and stir into a greased slow cooker. Cover and cook on low setting for 8 to 9 hours, or on high setting for 4 hours. Makes 8 servings.

Keep store-bought frozen, chopped onions on hand for slow-cooker recipes...it saves chopping time!

Peachy-Keen Sweet Potatoes

Tori Willis
Champaign, IL

The addition of peach pie filling makes these potatoes extra delicious.

2 lbs. sweet potatoes, peeled
   and cubed
1 c. peach pie filling

2 T. butter, melted
1/4 t. salt
1/4 t. pepper

Place sweet potatoes in a slow cooker that has been sprayed with non-stick vegetable spray. Add remaining ingredients; mix well. Cover and cook on low setting for 5 to 7 hours, until potatoes are tender when pierced with a fork. Serves 10.

Adding a simple ribbon drawstring to a farm-style sugar
sack turns it into a clever catch-all for mail,
clothespins or recipe cards.

Apple-Walnut Dressing

John Alexander
New Britain, CT

*Some call this dressing, others stuffing...whatever name
you choose, it's absolutely moist and delicious.*

1/2 c. butter, divided
1 c. chopped walnuts
2 onions, chopped
12-oz. pkg. herb-flavored
    stuffing mix

1-1/2 c. applesauce
1-1/2 c. water

Melt 2 tablespoons butter in a large skillet over medium heat.
Add walnuts and cook for about 5 minutes, until toasted, stirring
frequently. Remove from skillet; set aside. Melt remaining butter in
skillet. Add onions and cook for 3 for 4 minutes, until almost tender.
Spray a slow cooker with non-stick vegetable spray and add stuffing.
Stir in onions; mix gently. Add applesauce and water and mix gently.
Cover and cook on low setting for 4 to 5 hours. Sprinkle with toasted
nuts before serving. Makes 8 to 10 servings.

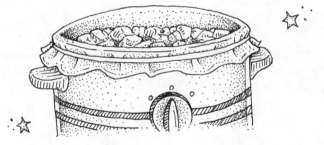

If a slow-cooker recipe calls for a spritz of non-stick vegetable
spray to the inside crock, try placing a disposable slow-cooker
liner inside instead...clean-up will be a breeze!

Not Your Mother's Green Beans

Cindy Neel
Gooseberry Patch

Roasted red peppers and Alfredo sauce...scrumptious additions!

28-oz. pkg. frozen cut green
  beans, thawed
1 onion, chopped
1 c. roasted red pepper strips,
  chopped
1/4 t. salt
1/8 t. pepper
10-oz. jar Alfredo sauce
2.8-oz. can French fried onions,
  divided

Combine all ingredients in a slow cooker, reserving half the French fried onions. Cover and cook on high setting for 3 to 4 hours, stirring after one hour. Just before serving, heat remaining French fried onions in a small skillet over medium heat for 2 to 3 minutes, stirring constantly. Stir casserole and sprinkle with heated onions. Serves 6 to 8.

Caramelized Onions

Shelley Turner
Boise, ID

So easy to make, these are a sweet, savory addition to any meal.

4 to 6 sweet onions, peeled   1/4 to 1/2 c. butter, diced

Cut top and bottoms from whole onions; place in a slow cooker. Top with the butter. Cover and cook on low setting for 10 to 12 hours, until golden and caramelized. Makes 6 to 8 servings.

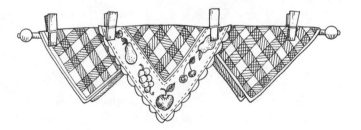

Savory Rice Pilaf

Cathy Hillier
Salt Lake City, UT

The blend of mushrooms, wild and brown rice make this a great side dish for beef, poultry, seafood or pork.

3/4 c. wild rice, uncooked
1/2 c. long-cooking brown rice, uncooked
1/2 lb. portabella mushrooms, sliced 1-inch thick

10-3/4 oz. can cream of mushroom with roasted garlic soup
1-1/2 c. water
1/8 t. pepper

Combine all ingredients in a slow cooker. Cover and cook on low setting for 6 to 7 hours, until rice is tender. Serves 6 to 8.

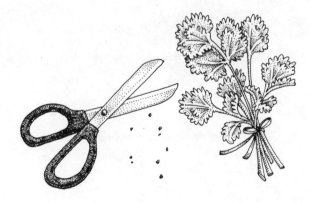

Fresh parsley is a great garnish for Savory Rice Pilaf.
Give parsley a quick rinse first...just swish back and forth
in cool water, shake and dry on paper towels.

Greek Potatoes

Jennifer Hagar
Providence Village, TX

I love Greek-style potatoes, and I wanted an easier way to cook them rather than in the oven. This slow-cooker version is absolutely delicious, and frees me up to do other activities while they simmer.

8 potatoes, peeled and sliced
   into wedges
1/2 c. olive oil
1 c. water

1 T. dried oregano
juice of 1 lemon
sea salt and pepper to taste
3 cloves garlic, minced

Combine all ingredients except garlic in a slow cooker; mix until potatoes are evenly coated. Stir in garlic. Cover and cook on low setting for 6 to 8 hours, or on high setting for 2 to 4 hours. If potatoes appear to be dry, add up to 1/2 cup additional water while cooking. Serves 6 to 8.

If the kids need a little snack to tide them over before dinner, whip up a tasty dip to serve with bagel chips. Blend together a packet of ranch salad dressing mix and 8 ounces of whipped cream cheese.

Garlic Smashed Potatoes

Nancy Girard
Chesapeake, VA

*This recipe has become one of our favorites and it's great
to make for those busy days.*

3 lbs. redskin potatoes, halved
   or quartered
4 cloves garlic, minced
2 T. olive oil
1 t. salt

1/2 c. water
1/2 c. cream cheese with chives
   and onions
1/4 to 1/2 c. milk

Place potatoes in a slow cooker. Add garlic, oil, salt and water; mix
well to coat potatoes. Cover and cook on high setting for 3-1/2 to
4-1/2 hours, until potatoes are tender. Mash potatoes with a potato
masher or fork. Stir in cream cheese until well blended; add enough
milk for soft consistency. Serve immediately, or keep warm in slow
cooker on low setting for up to 2 hours. Makes 4 to 6 servings.

Watching fireworks at a friend's house this year? Bring a
slow-cooker meal along with a red, white & blue basket
filled with snacks and dip mixes...an ideal hostess gift.

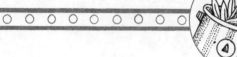

Dijon-Ginger Carrots

Angela Murphy
Tempe, AZ

A super simple, dressed-up carrot recipe...your family will love it.

12 carrots, peeled and sliced
1/3 c. Dijon mustard
1/2 c. brown sugar, packed
1 t. fresh ginger, peeled and
   minced

1/2 t. salt
1/8 t. pepper

Combine all ingredients in a slow cooker. Cover and cook on high setting for 2 to 3 hours, until carrots are tender, stirring twice during cooking. Makes 10 to 12 servings.

A step stool is oh-so handy in the kitchen...it's a snap to give it a perky new look with a fresh coat of paint.

Buttery Acorn Squash

Melody Taynor
Everett, WA

*Raisins, cinnamon, brown sugar and nutmeg...
a scrumptious fall-time recipe.*

3/4 c. brown sugar, packed
2 t. pumpkin pie spice
2 acorn squash, halved and
   seeded

3/4 c. raisins
1/4 c. butter
1/2 c. water

In a small bowl, combine brown sugar, cinnamon and nutmeg; spoon into squash halves. Sprinkle with raisins; dot with butter. Wrap each squash half individually in heavy-duty aluminum foil; seal tightly. Pour water into a slow cooker. Place squash, cut-side up, in slow cooker (packets may be stacked). Cover and cook on high setting for 4 hours, until squash is tender. Open foil packets carefully to allow steam to escape. Makes 4 servings.

A well-loved teapot that's been handed down makes a sweet flower vase. In spring, fill it with tulips, then in summer use zinnias. When fall arrives, tuck in colorful bittersweet and in winter sprigs of greenery and berries.

Angie's Macaroni & Cheese

Angie Stone
Argillite, KY

Comfort food at its best!

16-oz. pkg. elbow macaroni,
   uncooked
1 T. margarine, melted
12-oz. pkg. shredded Cheddar
   cheese

2 c. evaporated milk
Optional: 1/4 c. chopped onion,
   1/2 c. chopped green pepper

Measure out 3 cups macaroni, reserving remaining macaroni for
another recipe. Cook macaroni according to package directions; drain.
Combine macaroni and margarine; spread into a greased slow cooker.
Mix in remaining ingredients. Cover and cook on high setting for
2 to 3 hours. Makes 8 to 10 servings.

Kids love it when mac & cheese is on the dinner menu,
so before dinnertime rolls around, line the table with
kraft paper, pull out the crayons and let 'em decorate
the "tablecloth" any way they choose!

Broccoli, Cheese & Rice

Kelly Haught
Wellsville, OH

When I bring this, there's never anything left to take home from covered-dish dinners at church.

1 c. long-grain rice, cooked
16-oz. jar pasteurized process
  cheese sauce
2 10-3/4 oz. cans cream of
  chicken soup

2 16-oz. pkgs. frozen broccoli,
  thawed

Combine all ingredients in slow cooker. Cover and cook on low setting for 3 to 4 hours. Makes 6 to 8 servings.

When slow-cooker side dishes like Broccoli, Cheese & Rice are just about done, whip up a speedy chicken go-with. Simply pound chicken breasts until thin, coat both sides in flour and sprinkle on a bit of seasoning salt. Add a tablespoon of oil to a skilllet and cook for 3 minutes per side. Mmm!

Mama's Ranch Potatoes

Lisa Johnson
Hallsville, TX

*This recipe has been in my mama's recipe book for several years.
If I'm remembering right, it came from one of my aunts.*

2 lbs. redskin potatoes, peeled
  and quartered
8-oz. pkg. cream cheese,
  softened
1-oz. pkg. buttermilk ranch
  salad dressing mix

10-3/4 oz. can cream of potato
  soup
salt and pepper to taste

Place potatoes in a slow cooker. In a small bowl, combine cream
cheese and dressing mix; add soup and mix well. Add cream cheese
mixture to slow cooker; stir to combine. Cover and cook on low
setting for 7 hours, or on high setting for 3-1/2 hours. Before serving,
stir to blend. Makes about 6 servings.

Keep the week's menu and shopping list right at your fingertips.
Tack a length of wide rick-rack to the bulletin board,
and just slip lists underneath...so handy!

Tomatoes & Green Beans

Jennifer Swartz
Smithville, TX

*An old-fashioned dish that's as delicious now as it was
in Grandma's day.*

2 14-1/2 oz. cans green beans,
   drained
14-1/2 oz. can stewed tomatoes

5 slices bacon, crisply cooked
   and crumbled

Combine all ingredients in a slow cooker; cover and cook on low
setting for 3 to 4 hours. Serves 4.

Instead of a sit-down dinner with friends, plan a casual
get-together. Potlucks are so easy to plan...everyone brings
along their favorite dish to share.

Mock Pierogies

Kelly Ziemba
Port Saint Lucie, FL

This is a wonderful, flavorful casserole that tastes just like potato and cheese pierogies...without all the fuss!

1/2 c. butter, melted
1 c. onion, chopped
6 to 7 potatoes, peeled, cubed
   and cooked

16-oz. pkg. shredded Cheddar
   cheese, divided
16-oz. pkg. bowtie pasta,
   cooked

Combine butter and onion in a slow cooker; add potatoes. Sprinkle with half the cheese. Spread pasta on top; sprinkle with remaining cheese. Cover and cook on low setting for 30 to 40 minutes, stirring occasionally. Serves 6 to 8.

Everyone in the family will love to decorate their own cupcake for dessert tonight. Set out the frosting, sprinkles and candies, then let the fun begin!

Fantastic Potatoes

Samantha Sparks
Madison, WI

Creamy and cheesy...what more could you ask for?

10-3/4 oz. can cream of
   mushroom with roasted
   garlic soup
8-oz. container sour cream

1-1/2 c. shredded Colby Jack
   cheese
32-oz. pkg. frozen diced
   potatoes, divided

Combine soup, sour cream and cheese in a medium bowl; mix well. Spread half the potatoes in a slow cooker that has been sprayed with non-stick vegetable spray. Top with half of soup mixture. Layer on remaining potatoes and top with remaining soup mixture. Cover and cook on high setting for 3-1/2 to 4-1/2 hours. Serves 8 to 10.

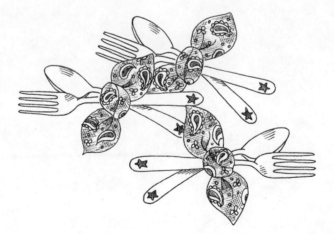

Give tonight's table a little flair...knot a cheery bandanna around each set of flatware. Bandannas come in so many bright colors, everyone can choose their own favorite.

Twist & Shout Pasta

Barb Sulser
Gooseberry Patch

We giggle over the name, but the kids do shout for joy when they know I'm serving this!

2 c. half-and-half
10-3/4 oz. can Cheddar
   cheese soup
1/2 c. butter, melted

16-oz. pkg. shredded Cheddar
   cheese
16-oz. pkg. rotini pasta, cooked

In a slow cooker, blend half-and-half, soup and butter until smooth; stir in cheese and pasta. Cover and cook on low setting for 2-1/2 hours, or until cheese is melted. Makes 12 to 15 servings.

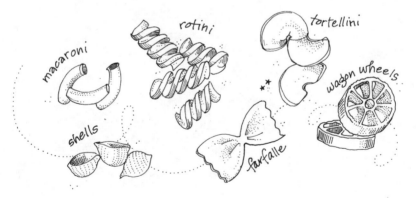

Mix up a favorite noodle recipe by substituting different types of pasta. Check out the grocer's for bowties, wagon wheels, shells or alphabet shapes.

Easy Rice Pilaf

Brenda Thompson
Athens, OH

This is so easy to prepare as well as filling...it's a great addition to any meal.

1/2 c. butter, softened
6 c. beef broth
4 c. long-grain rice, uncooked

8-oz. pkg. mushrooms, diced
1.35-oz. pkg. onion soup mix

Grease slow cooker with butter. Place remaining butter in slow cooker. Add remaining ingredients; stir to mix. Cover and cook on high setting for 2 to 3 hours. Makes 16 servings.

Enjoy the little things, for one day you may look back
and realize they were the big things.

-Robert Brault

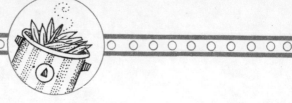

Ham & Escalloped Potatoes

Judi Candler
Ridgeway, OH

*This recipe is one I turn to when someone is feeling under the weather,
as it's easy to make-and-take in my slow cooker.*

4 slices baked ham
4 potatoes, peeled and sliced
1 onion, sliced
10-3/4 oz. can cream of
   mushroom soup

8-oz. pkg. shredded Cheddar
   cheese, divided
Optional: paprika to taste

Layer ham, potatoes, onion and cheese in a slow cooker, reserving
1/2 cup cheese for topping. Pour soup over cheese; sprinkle with
paprika, if desired, and cover with 1/2 cup cheese. Cover and cook
on low setting for 8 hours, or on high setting for 4 hours.
Serves 4 to 6.

Add a touch of whimsy! A vintage child's sand pail or
watering can can hold kitchen utensils.

Lakeside Casserole

Kathy Grashoff
Fort Wayne, IN

*It's nice you can use the slow cooker in any kind of weather,
especially summer, because you don't heat up your kitchen...
more time to be out on the lake!*

1 lb. ground pork sausage,
   cooked and drained
1-1/2 oz. pkg. chicken noodle
   soup mix
1/4 c. long-grain rice, cooked

1 stalk celery, diced
1/3 c. slivered almonds
4 c. water
salt to taste

Combine all ingredients in a lightly greased slow cooker; stir well.
Cover and cook on low setting for 6 to 10 hours, or on high setting
for 2 to 3 hours, until rice is tender. Serves 4.

A wire egg basket makes sharing the extra bounty from
your garden so easy...they're strong and roomy. Don't
forget to tuck in a few favorite recipes!

Onion-Topped Potato Casserole

*Tina Dammrich
Saint Louis, MO*

This is always a favorite take-along recipe.

32-oz. pkg. frozen diced
   potatoes, thawed
2 10-3/4 oz. cans Cheddar
   cheese soup

12-oz. can evaporated milk
salt and pepper to taste
2.8-oz. can French fried onions,
   divided

In a large bowl, combine potatoes, soup, evaporated milk, salt,
pepper and half the onions; pour into a greased slow cooker. Cover
and cook on low setting for 8 to 9 hours, or on high setting for
4 hours. Sprinkle with remaining onions just before serving.
Makes 8 servings.

For variety, drizzle servings of Onion-Topped Potato Casserole
with a bit of chipotle sauce...it adds a great spicy flavor.

Simply Delicious Potatoes

Tasha Friesen
Liberal, KS

Sometimes I use the hot Mexican cheese spread to add spice.

32-oz. pkg. frozen diced
  potatoes, thawed
26-oz. can cream of
  chicken soup
16-oz. container sour cream

8-oz. pkg. shredded sharp
  Cheddar cheese
8-oz. pkg. pasteurized process
  cheese spread, diced

Combine all ingredients in a slow cooker; mix well. Cover and cook on high setting for about 2 hours, until hot and bubbly. Makes 10 to 12 servings.

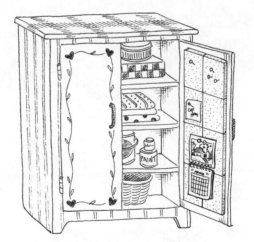

Keep those take-out menus handy...line the inside of
a cabinet door with self-stick cork tiles to make the
easiest-ever bulletin board.

Super-Simple Squash

Kay Marone
Des Moines, IA

*I always make squash this way...you can also use soy sauce
or water instead of Worcestershire sauce.*

2 lbs. winter squash, halved and   1 T. Worcestershire sauce
    seeds removed

Place squash in a slow cooker; drizzle with Worcestershire sauce.
Cover and cook on low setting until squash is easily pierced through,
about 4 to 6 hours. Serves 4.

When cooking a large squash, remember that any extra will
freeze well and also makes a yummy "pumpkin" pie.

Little Extras

Italian Scallion Meatballs

Wendy Jacobs
Idaho Falls, ID

A classic recipe you can be sure everyone will love. I like to garnish the meatballs with a sprinkling of chopped scallions before serving.

1 c. grape juice
1 c. apple jelly
1 c. catsup

8-oz. can tomato sauce
4 lbs. frozen Italian-style
   meatballs

In a small saucepan, combine all ingredients except meatballs. Cook and stir over medium heat until jelly is melted; remove from heat. Place meatballs in a slow cooker; pour sauce over top and gently stir to coat. Cover and cook on low setting for 4 hours. Makes about 11 dozen.

Did you know April is National Garden Month? Dress up some terra cotta pots with acrylic paint...it's easy. When the paint is completely dry, top it off with a matte spray sealant.

Aloha Sausage Links

Barb Stout
Gooseberry Patch

A neighbor hosted a luau party this summer and these tasty sausages were on the menu...I had to have the recipe!

2 lbs. smoked pork sausage
   links, sliced 1/2-inch thick
8-oz. bottle Catalina salad
   dressing

8-oz. bottle Russian salad
   dressing
1/2 c. brown sugar, packed
1/2 c. pineapple juice

Brown sausage in a skillet over medium heat; drain and place in a slow cooker. Add dressings, sugar and juice to skillet; cook and stir over medium-low heat until sugar is dissolved. Pour over sausage. Cover and cook on low setting for one to 2 hours. Makes 16 servings.

Summertime Salsa

Zoe Bennett
Columbia, SC

The slow cooker is a super way to make homemade salsa... with so little effort!

10 plum tomatoes, cored
2 cloves garlic
1 onion, cut into wedges

2 jalapeño peppers, seeded
1/4 c. fresh cilantro
Optional: 1/2 t. salt

Cut a small slit in 2 tomatoes; insert a garlic clove into each. Place all tomatoes and onion in a slow cooker. Cover and cook on high setting for 2-1/2 to 3 hours, until vegetables are tender; cool. Combine tomato mixture, cilantro and salt, if using, in a blender or food processor. Process until smooth. Serve immediately or refrigerate until ready to serve. Makes about 2 cups.

Texas Queso Dip

Amy Shilliday
Tampa, FL

*Everyone will love this dip...once they sample it, be ready
to share the recipe!*

1 lb. hot ground pork sausage,
  browned and drained
32-oz. pkg. pasteurized
  process cheese spread, cubed

10-oz. can tomatoes with chiles
1/2 c. milk
corn chips

Combine all ingredients except chips in a slow cooker. Cover and cook
on low setting until cheese is melted, about 2 hours. Serve with corn
chips. Makes 20 to 24 servings.

Invite friends & neighbors
over for an old-fashioned
barbecue. While the kids
are tossing a football,
and before the grill
heats up, load a picnic
table with slow-cooker
appetizers to nibble on...
meatballs, dips, fondue
and sausages are
just the thing!

Spicy Tailgate Dip

Amanda Mervicker
Austin, TX

Try serving this dip in a hollowed-out round loaf of sourdough.

1 lb. ground pork sausage,
   browned and drained
2 8-oz. pkgs. cream cheese,
   cubed

10-oz. can tomatoes with chiles
corn chips

Combine all ingredients except chips in slow cooker. Cover and cook on low setting for one to 2 hours, until heated through and cream cheese is melted. Serve with corn chips. Serves 16 to 20.

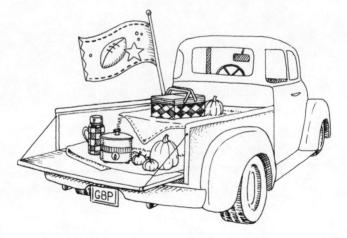

Tailgate in style...fly a family flag over your tailgating spot so it's easy for friends & family to find you. Cut a length of fabric, then let the little ones get creative with fabric paint and glitter glue. A one-of-a-kind creation!

Just Peachy Cider

Jennie Gist
Gooseberry Patch

While on vacation, we ran across this little farm stand with all varieties of cider...black bing cherry, peach and cinnamon apple. They also carried jams, jellies, syrups and honey...it was such fun to stock up on food gifts to bring home. This recipe is one shared with us by a good friend...I hope you enjoy it as much as we do.

4 5-1/2 oz. cans peach nectar   3/4 t. pumpkin pie spice
2 c. apple juice   4 slices orange

In a slow cooker, combine nectar, juice and pumpkin pie spice; top with orange slices. Cover and cook on low setting for 4 to 6 hours. Stir before serving. Serves 4.

Juice bottles and jar lids can be tricky to open. Wrap a rubber band around the lid several times...the little extra grip it provides makes the lid a snap to twist off!

Warm Fruity Punch

Virginia Watson
Scranton, PA

Serve up mugs of this warm-you-up punch after a family outing in the frosty air.

32-oz. bottle cranberry juice
  cocktail
32-oz. can pineapple juice
1/3 c. red cinnamon candies

4-inch cinnamon stick
Optional: additional cinnamon
  sticks

Combine juices, candies and cinnamon stick in a slow cooker. Cover and cook on low setting for 2 to 5 hours. Remove cinnamon stick before serving. Use additional cinnamon sticks as stirrers, if desired. Makes 8 servings.

When time is short, a super-fast dessert is in order.
Fill sundae cups with cubes of angel food cake
layered with pie filling...yummy!

Pepperoni Dip

Crystal Branstrom
Russell, PA

Who can pass up the flavor of pepperoni in a dip? It's a winner!

10-3/4 oz. can cream of
  celery soup
6-oz. pkg. pepperoni, chopped

8-oz. pkg. cream cheese,
  softened and cubed
assorted crackers

Combine all ingredients in a slow cooker. Cover and cook on low setting for one to 2 hours. Serve with crackers. Makes 8 to 10 servings.

Purchasing a new slow cooker? Look for one that has a "warm" setting...it's perfect for keeping dips toasty throughout potlucks and parties.

Mama's Pizza Fondue

Angie Venable
Gooseberry Patch

When we want the taste of our favorite pizza, this scrumptious fondue is what we make.

29-oz. jar meatless spaghetti
   sauce
8-oz. pkg. shredded mozzarella
   cheese
1/4 c. shredded Parmesan
   cheese

2 t. dried oregano
1 t. dried, minced onion
Optional: 1/4 t. garlic powder
1 loaf Italian bread, cubed

In a slow cooker, combine all ingredients except bread. Cover and cook for 4 to 6 hours, until cheese is melted and sauce is hot. Serve with bread cubes. Makes about 4 cups.

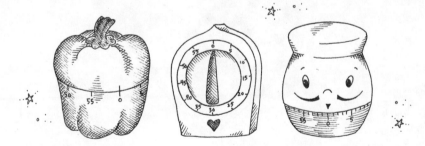

Make it a meal. Try adding a pound of browned ground beef or Italian sausage to Mama's Pizza Fondue. Add warm bread sticks for dipping and a spinach salad...a speedy supper!

Shari's Reuben Dip

Shari Flatt
Dubuque, IA

All the flavor of a favorite sandwich in a warm dip...amazing!

16-oz. pkg. shredded Swiss
    cheese
1/2 c. Thousand Island salad
    dressing

1 lb. deli corned beef, chopped
10-oz. pkg. sauerkraut, drained
1 loaf sliced party rye

Combine all ingredients except party rye in a slow cooker. Cover and cook on high setting for 45 minutes, until hot and bubbly. Serve with party rye. Serves 8 to 10.

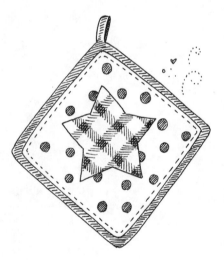

A recipe card holder that you didn't know you had!
Place your recipe card in the knife-sharpener side of
an electric can opener. It keeps the card clean
and at the perfect height for reading.

Mom's Kielbasa

Tiffany Brinkley
Broomfield, CO

Our family cans homemade applesauce and apple pie filling every fall. One year, we had a contest to see who could create a brand new recipe using either one...this one was the winner, hands down!

2 lbs. Kielbasa, sliced
  1-inch thick
3/4 c. brown sugar, packed

1 c. chunky applesauce
2 cloves garlic, minced

Mix together all ingredients in a slow cooker. Cover and cook on low setting for 6 to 8 hours. Makes 12 servings.

Make a trip to the apple orchard a family event this year. You'll bring home baskets of crisp apples, jugs of tangy apple cider...perfect for fall slow cooking.

Shauna's Apple Butter

Shauna Brooks
Parkville, MD

This is a BIG hit with family and neighbors!

5-1/2 lbs. Cortland or Gala
   apples, cored, peeled and
   cubed
2 c. sugar
2 t. cinnamon

1/4 t. ground cloves
1/4 t. salt
4 1-pt. canning jars and lids,
   sterilized

Place apples in a slow cooker. In a medium bowl, mix together sugar, cinnamon, cloves and salt; pour over apples and mix well. Cover and cook on high setting for one hour. Reduce heat to low setting and cook for 9 to 11 hours, stirring occasionally, until thickened and dark brown. Uncover and continue cooking on low setting for an additional hour. Stir with a whisk until desired consistency is reached. Spoon into hot sterilized jars, leaving 1/4-inch headspace. Wipe rims; secure with lids and rings. Process in a boiling water bath for 10 minutes; set jars on a towel to cool. Check for seals. Makes 4 pints.

Celebrate Johnny Appleseed's birthday on September 26th...
it's a tasty reason to enjoy an apple treat of any kind!

Peach Butter

Lisa Hays
Crocker, MO

Spread on warm biscuits...what a way to begin the day!

6 c. peaches, pitted, peeled and
    sliced
3 c. sugar

1-1/2 c. apricot nectar
2 T. orange or lemon juice
1 t. vanilla extract

Put peaches through a food mill or purée in a food processor. Combine peaches and remaining ingredients; mix well and pour into a slow cooker. Cover and cook on low setting for 3 hours. Uncover and continue cooking until thickened, about 5 to 8 hours. Keep refrigerated. Makes about 1-1/2 pints.

Applesauce

Gloria Smith
Webster, MA

I like to use Granny Smith apples for this recipe.

3 lbs. apples, cored, peeled and
    sliced
1/2 c. brown sugar, packed

1 t. cinnamon
1-1/2 T. lemon juice

Combine all ingredients in a slow cooker. Cover and cook on high setting for 3 hours. Stir occasionally; mash with potato masher until desired consistency. Makes 6 to 8 servings.

It isn't the great big pleasures that count the most;
it's making a great deal out of the little ones.

-Unknown

Beefy Broccoli Dip

Shelley Turner
Boise, ID

This dip is one I always make when it's family game night.

1 lb. ground beef, browned
   and drained
16-oz. pkg. pasteurized process
   cheese spread, cubed
10-3/4 oz. can cream of
   mushroom soup

10-oz. pkg. frozen chopped
   broccoli, thawed
2 T. salsa
tortilla chips

Combine all ingredients except tortilla chips; mix well. Cover and cook on low setting for 2 to 3 hours, until heated through, stirring after one hour. Serve with tortilla chips. Makes 5-1/2 cups.

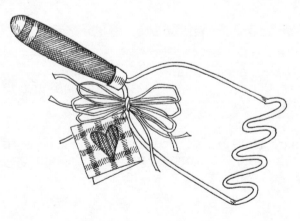

An easy way to crumble ground beef...use a potato masher.
It makes browning so quick & easy.

Creamy Hot Corn Dip

Tanya Miller
Millersburg, OH

*The last time I made this dip, people were eating it with spoons
instead of over nachos! My husband calls this dip "man food!"*

2 8-oz. pkgs. cream cheese,
  softened
2 15-1/4 oz. cans corn, drained

1/2 c. butter
2 jalapeño peppers, diced
tortilla chips

Combine all ingredients except chips in a slow cooker. Cover and
cook on high setting for 30 minutes; stir until smooth. Reduce setting
to low to keep warm. The longer it cooks, the spicier it will get. Serve
hot with tortilla chips. Makes about 15 servings.

Make your own "baked" tortilla chips...it's easy. Spritz both
sides of corn tortillas with non-stick cooking spray. Cut into
wedges and microwave on high setting for 5 to 6 minutes,
turning wedges over every 1-1/2 minutes. Sprinkle warm
chips with sea salt and serve.

Game-Day Apple Cider

Elizabeth Blackstone
Racine, WI

Sips of this cider will warm you up during those late-season football games when it can be so chilly.

8 whole cloves
4 c. apple cider
4 c. pineapple juice

1/2 c. water
4-inch cinnamon stick
1 teabag

Place cloves on a double thickness of cheesecloth; bring up corners of cloth and tie with kitchen string to form a bag. Place remaining ingredients in a slow cooker; add spice bag. Cover and cook on low setting for 2 hours, or until cider reaches desired temperature. Discard spice bag, cinnamon stick and teabag before serving. Makes 8 servings.

Serve up cider paired with this yummy dip for apple slices. Blend together an 8-ounce package of softened cream cheese with 6 tablespoons packed brown sugar and 1/2 teaspoon cinnamon.

Witches' Brew

Lynda Robson
Boston, MA

*Because the color is dark, this is the recipe I use when my little
trick-or-treaters need to warm up after haunting the neighborhood
on a chilly October night.*

5 lbs. Concord grapes
8 c. water, divided
1-1/2 c. sugar

8 whole cloves
4 4-inch cinnamon sticks
1/8 t. nutmeg

In a large saucepan or Dutch oven, combine grapes and 2 cups water.
Bring to a boil over medium heat, stirring constantly. Press through a
strainer; reserve juice and discard skins and seeds. Pour juice through
a double layer of cheesecloth into a slow cooker. Add sugar, cloves,
cinnamon sticks, nutmeg and remaining water. Cover and cook on
low setting for 3 hours. Discard cloves and cinnamon sticks before
serving. Makes 10 to 12 servings.

Dress up servings of pumpkin pie with black plastic spider
rings...have kids remove the "spiders" and slip 'em on
before enjoying their tricky treat!

Seashore Crab Dip

Ursula Juarez-Wall
Dumfries, VA

Keep the seashore theme going and create a crab canoe...just spoon the dip into an oblong shaped loaf of crusty bread!

6-oz. can crabmeat, drained
8-oz. pkg. cream cheese,
   softened and cubed
1/2 c. butter, sliced

2 T. white wine or water
1/8 t. seafood seasoning
bagel chips or crackers

Combine all ingredients except bagel chips or crackers in a mini slow cooker. Cover and cook on low setting for about one hour; stir gently. Serve with bagel chips or crackers. Serves 6 to 8.

Fill the summertime picnic table with whimsies...alongside Seashore Crab Dip, serve oyster crackers and fish-shaped crackers, watch tealights sparkle in Mason jars filled with sea glass and serve fruit or tossed salads in new sand pails.

Our Favorite Fondue

Jamie Johnson
Gooseberry Patch

*Nothing could be more simple to prepare...this fondue is a
must-have when I get together with friends.*

1-1/2 to 2 c. milk
2 8-oz. pkgs. cream cheese,
  softened

1-1/2 c. grated Parmesan cheese
1/2 t. garlic salt
1 loaf French bread, cubed

In a large saucepan, cook and stir milk and cream cheese over low
heat until cream cheese is melted. Stir in Parmesan cheese and garlic
salt; cook and stir until heated through. Transfer to a slow cooker;
keep warm. Serve with bread cubes. Makes 3-1/2 cups.

Offer a variety of breads when sharing your favorite fondue.
Rosemary-garlic, tomato-basil, sourdough, focaccia,
ciabatta and sesame all have unique flavors...you just
might discover a new favorite.

Speedy Sausages

Denice Louk
Garnett, KS

These sausages are ready in just an hour.

16-oz. pkg. mini smoked
   sausages
Optional: 1/2 c. bourbon

1/2 c. grape jelly
2 c. catsup
1/2 c. brown sugar, packed

Combine all ingredients together in a slow cooker. Cook on high setting for one hour. Makes 10 to 12 servings.

Place unfolded maps on the table...a super-fast, super-fun tablecloth!

All-American Hamburger Dip

Cathy Gilliland
Rose Hill, IA

Enjoy this dip whenever you want a savory snack...tailgating, neighborhood block parties or during family movie night.

1 lb. ground beef, browned and drained
16-oz. pkg. pasteurized process cheese spread, cubed

14-1/2 oz. can tomatoes with chiles
1/8 t. ground cumin
tortilla chips

Combine all ingredients except chips in a slow cooker. Cover and cook on high setting until cheese is melted, about 30 minutes; stir occasionally. Reduce to low setting to serve. Serve with tortilla chips. Serves 6 to 8.

It's time for a bike ride...wind ribbons in the bike spokes, pump up the tires and fill the bike basket with binoculars, snacks and a camera. Find a country road and enjoy!

Chicken-Chili Con Queso Dip

Shannon Young
Churubusco, IN

This is a must for all family gatherings at my home. Everyone asks, "Are you making your chicken dip?"

2 boneless, skinless chicken breasts, cooked and shredded
32-oz. pkg. pasteurized process cheese spread, cubed

8-oz. pkg. cream cheese, cubed
16-oz. jar salsa
4-oz. can diced green chiles
tortilla chips

Combine all ingredients except tortilla chips in a slow cooker. Cover and cook on high setting for 1-1/2 to 2 hours, until cheese is melted, stirring occasionally. Reduce to low setting to serve. Serve with tortilla chips. Serves 12.

When a favorite photo is smaller than the frame, fill up the space by placing a vintage hankie or postcard behind the photo...how sweet.

Cheesy Mexican Bean Dip

Amy DeLamar Smith
Newport News, VA

If you are like me, you always wonder what to fix with tacos. Well, this is the perfect side dish. This is also a great appetizer for parties. Just put a big bowl of tortilla chips next to the slow cooker and let your guests help themselves!

31-oz. can refried beans
10-3/4 oz. can nacho cheese
  soup
1 c. salsa
1 t. salt

1/4 c. green onion, chopped
8-oz. pkg. shredded Cheddar
  cheese
tortilla chips

In a large bowl, combine beans, soup, salsa and salt. Pour into a slow cooker. Cover and cook on low setting for 3-1/2 hours. Sprinkle with green onion and cheese. Cover and cook for an additional 10 minutes, or until cheese is melted. Serve with tortilla chips. Makes 6 to 8 servings.

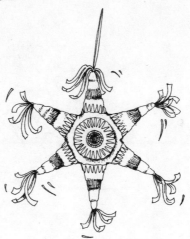

While dinner is preparing itself in the slow cooker,
enjoy a scavenger hunt. Hide surprises throughout the yard,
make a list of clues and send the kids on their way.
When they return, have a piñata waiting for them!

Championship Cheese Dip

David Wink
Gooseberry Patch

*A few years ago, I whipped this up before our biggest football
rivalry game. We won the game, and went on to win the
National Championship. Now, I make it for every game!*

1 lb. ground beef, browned
  and drained
1/2 lb. spicy pork sausage,
  browned and drained
32-oz. pkg. pasteurized process
  cheese spread, cubed

2 10-oz. cans tomatoes with
  chiles
tortilla chips

Combine all ingredients except chips in a slow cooker; mix well.
Cover and cook on low setting for 4 hours, or until the cheese is
melted, stirring occasionally. Serve with tortilla chips. Makes
20 to 25 servings.

Show your hometown spirit...cheer on the high school
football team with a Friday neighborhood block party. Invite
neighbors to bring along their favorite appetizer to share
and don't forget to wear school colors!

Nacho Cheese Dip

Sheri Saly
Leesburg, VA

This dip goes fast at football game parties!

32-oz. pkg. pasteurized process
   cheese spread, cubed
1-1/2 lbs. ground beef, browned
   and drained

10-3/4 oz. can cream of
   mushroom soup
16-oz. jar salsa
tortilla chips

Melt cheese in a microwave-safe bowl, stirring every minute until melted. Combine cheese and remaining ingredients except chips in a slow cooker. Cover and cook on high setting for about one hour. Turn down to low setting to keep dip warm. Serve with tortilla chips. Makes 20 to 25 servings.

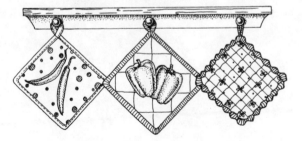

A paste made of equal parts cream of tartar and vinegar is
a great mixture for removing stains on a slow cooker.
Just rub on, then rinse well.

Hot Spiced Apple Cider

Colleen Nieland
Omaha, NE

*I think of warm holiday mornings whenever I smell
the aroma of this wonderful cider.*

1 to 2 T. whole cloves
1 orange

3 4-inch cinnamon sticks
1 gal. apple juice

Press cloves into skin of orange, completely covering orange. Place orange and cinnamon sticks in a slow cooker. Pour in apple juice; cover and cook on low setting for 4 to 6 hours, until hot. Makes one gallon.

Nothing beats the chill like warm cider...add some orange
or lemon rind twists for a real treat.

Breakfasts

Country Cabin Potatoes

Carol Lytle
Columbus, OH

Our family stayed in a beautiful 1800's log cabin in southern Ohio one fall. Not only was it peaceful and relaxing, but breakfast was brought to our door each morning...what a treat!

4 14-1/2 oz. cans sliced
  potatoes, drained
2 10-3/4 oz. cans cream
  of celery

16-oz. container sour cream
10 slices bacon, crisply cooked
  and crumbled
6 green onions, thinly sliced

Place potatoes in a slow cooker. Combine remaining ingredients; pour over potatoes and mix well. Cover and cook on high setting for 4 to 5 hours. Makes 12 servings.

For a speedy breakfast, keep all the ingredients in one spot for favorite slow-cooker recipes

Sunrise Hashbrowns

Amy Butcher
Columbus, GA

Absolutely the best served with eggs sunny-side-up,
crispy bacon and biscuits topped with honey butter.

28-oz. pkg. frozen diced
  potatoes
2 c. cooked ham, cubed
2-oz. jar diced pimentos,
  drained

10-3/4 oz. can Cheddar cheese
  soup
3/4 c. milk
1/4 t. pepper

In a slow cooker, combine potatoes, ham and pimentos. In a bowl, combine soup, milk and pepper; pour over potato mixture. Cover and cook on low setting for 6 to 8 hours. Serves 4.

On a frosty morning, send your socks on a quick
tumble through the dryer...ahhh.

Berry Bog Oatmeal

Elizabeth Blackstone
Racine, WI

*Cranberries and a touch of honey turn ordinary oatmeal
into breakfast the whole family looks forward to.*

1 c. steel-cut oats, uncooked
1 c. sweetened, dried cranberries
1 c. chopped dates

4 c. water
1/2 c. half-and-half
2 T. honey

Combine oats, cranberries, dates and water in a greased slow cooker.
Cover and cook on low setting for 6 to 8 hours. Stir in half-and-half
and honey. Serves 4.

Keep in mind if half-and-half isn't in the fridge,
an equal amount of evaporated milk can be substituted.

Grammy's Porridge

*April Jacobs
Loveland, CO*

*Raisins and apples seem to be made for each other, and in this
homestyle porridge, they absolutely taste terrific together.*

1/4 c. cracked wheat, uncooked
3/4 c. long-cooking oats,
   uncooked
3 c. water
1/2 c. raisins

1/4 c. wheat germ
1/2 c. apple, cored, peeled and
   grated
Garnish: cinnamon, milk, honey

Combine all ingredients except garnish in a slow cooker. Cover and
cook on low setting for 6 to 8 hours, or overnight. Spoon into serving
bowls and serve with cinnamon, milk and honey. Makes 4 servings.

Orange marmalade or a swirl of strawberry jam is a great
stir-in to your morning bowl of oatmeal.

Apple Pie Bread Pudding

Kim Faulkner
Gooseberry Patch

We made apple pie jam last September, so we thought, why not try pie filling in a bread pudding recipe? I'm glad we did...it's a scrumptious breakfast treat.

3 eggs, beaten
2 c. milk
1/2 c. sugar
21-oz. can apple pie filling

6-1/2 c. cinnamon-raisin bread, cubed
Optional: whipped cream

In a large bowl, whisk together eggs, milk and sugar. Gently stir in pie filling and bread cubes; pour mixture into a lightly greased slow cooker. Cover and cook on low setting for 3 hours, until a knife inserted near center comes out clean. Remove crock from cooker, if possible, or turn off cooker. Let stand, uncovered, for 30 to 45 minutes to cool slightly before serving. Spoon bread pudding into serving bowls. If desired, top each serving with a dollop of whipped cream. Makes 6 servings.

Surprise Mom with breakfast in bed...and it doesn't
have to be just on Mothers' Day!

Sweetie Banana Oatmeal

Athena Colegrove
Big Springs, TX

My little ones, with Daddy's help, made this for me on Valentine's Day...
what a yummy breakfast surprise from my 3 sweeties!

2 c. long-cooking oats,
  uncooked
1/2 c. sweetened condensed
  milk

4 c. water
2 bananas, thinly sliced

Combine oats, milk and water in a slow cooker that has been sprayed
with non-stick vegetable spray. Cover and cook on low setting for
6 to 8 hours. Add bananas 10 to 15 minutes before serving. Makes
4 servings.

Pumpkin Oatmeal

Shannon James
Georgetown, KY

I have 4 small children, so my love for cooking can only come out late
at night once they have gone to bed. This is always a favorite in the fall
and around the holidays. Who doesn't love waking up to the sweet and
spicy aroma of pumpkin baking?

2 c. long-cooking oats,
  uncooked
1 c. canned pumpkin pie filling
2 c. milk
2 c. water

1/4 c. butter
1/2 t. salt
Garnish: whipped cream,
  maple syrup

Mix together all ingredients except garnish in a lightly greased slow
cooker. Cover and cook on low setting 8 hours. Serve with a dollop
of whipped cream or a drizzle of maple syrup. Makes 6 to 8 servings.

Farmhouse Applesauce

Jill Valentine
Jackson, TN

I just love this applesauce served over homemade pancakes or waffles.

8 to 10 tart apples, cored, peeled
   and cut into chunks
1/2 to 1 c. sugar

1/2 c. water
1 t. cinnamon

Combine apples, sugar, water and cinnamon in a slow cooker; stir gently. Cover and cook on low setting for 6 to 8 hours, until apples are tender. Makes 6 servings.

Bring along a slow-cooker meal to a new mom or a girls' book club meeting...as soon as you arrive, just plug it back in to keep warm. So simple!

Ranch House Breakfast

Rita Morgan
Pueblo, CO

*Our family went out west to spend a week on a Texas ranch...
we had a ball! And no kidding, every morning, straight from
the chuck wagon, a breakfast very similar to this was served.*

3 qts. boiling water
2 T. salt
2 t. pepper
5 c. steel-cut oats, uncooked
2 lbs. ground beef

2 lbs. ground pork breakfast
   sausage
2 onions, finely chopped
1/4 c. oil

Combine water, salt and pepper in a slow cooker. Stir in oats; cover
and cook on high setting for 1-1/2 hours. In a large bowl, mix
together beef, pork, and onions; stir into oat mixture. Cover and
cook on low setting for 3 hours, stirring occasionally. Transfer to a
13"x9" baking pan; cool until firm. Turn out onto wax paper and chill
for one hour. Cut into thin slices. Heat oil in a large, heavy skillet over
medium-high heat. Fry slices until golden. Makes 20 servings.

Sit loosely in the saddle of life.
-Robert Louis Stevenson

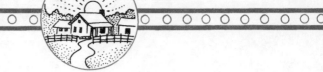

Blueberry Breakfast Cake

Beth Kramer
Port Saint Lucie, FL

If you like moist blueberry muffins, you're gonna love this cake.

6-1/2 oz. pkg. blueberry muffin
   mix
1/4 c. milk

1 egg
1/8 t. cinnamon

Reserve 1/4 cup muffin mix; set aside. Spray a slow cooker with
non-stick vegetable spray. Stir together remaining muffin mix, milk,
egg and cinnamon just until combined; spoon into slow cooker,
spreading evenly. Cover top of slow cooker with 6 to 8 paper towels
to absorb condensation. Cover and cook on high setting for one hour.
Turn off slow cooker and let stand for 10 minutes. Loosen edges
of cake with a knife. Place a plate on top of slow cooker; invert to
remove. Place another plate on top of cake and invert again. Slice
into wedges. Serves 6.

Make breakfast fun for kids, especially on school days.
Cut the centers from a slice of toast with a cookie cutter,
serve milk or juice with twisty straws or put a smiley face
on a bagel using raisins and cream cheese.

Caramel-Nut Rolls

Jamie Moffatt
French Lick, IN

These rolls slowly bake in a coffee can set inside a slow cooker.

1/2 c. brown sugar, packed
1/4 c. chopped nuts
2 8-oz. tubes refrigerated
   biscuits

1/4 c. butter, melted
Garnish: cinnamon, sugar

Combine brown sugar and nuts in a small bowl. Dip each biscuit into butter, then into brown sugar mixture. Arrange biscuits in a greased 3-pound metal coffee can or a slow-cooker cake pan insert. Sprinkle each layer of biscuits lightly with cinnamon and sugar. Place can or pan in slow cooker; if using a coffee can, cover with several layers of paper towels. Cover and cook on high setting for 3 to 4 hours. Makes 10 to 12 servings.

Deliver a batch of Caramel-Nut Rolls to the local firehouse, or wrap up several and tuck in the mailbox for your letter carrier...what a great way to start the day.

Grits with Gusto

Penny Sherman
Cumming, GA

*If you like breakfast a little spicy... sprinkle warm grits with
a tablespoon or two of shredded cheese and dollop a spoonful
of hot salsa right in the middle.*

2 c. long-cooking grits,
  uncooked
6 c. water
4-oz. can chopped green chiles
1 jalapeño pepper, seeded and
  finely chopped

1/8 t. cayenne pepper
1 t. salt
Optional: 1/2 t. paprika,
  1/2 t. chili powder
Garnish: butter, salt and pepper

Combine all ingredients except garnish in a lightly greased slow
cooker; mix well. Cover and cook on low setting for about 8 hours.
Stir after first hour of cooking; stir well before serving. Serve with
butter, salt and pepper. Makes 6 servings.

Add a splash of color to the breakfast table...it wakes everyone
up! Mix & match cheery plates, set out spunky retro
juice glasses and arrange sunny marigolds and
red-hot zinnias together in a vase.

South-of-the-Border Breakfast

Jo Ann

For a new flavor, try peach or pineapple salsa as a garnish.

1 lb. ground pork breakfast
  sausage, browned and
  drained
4-oz. can chopped green chiles
1 c. frozen peppers and onions,
  thawed and drained

2-1/2 c. shredded Monterey Jack
  or Pepper Jack cheese
1-1/2 doz. eggs, beaten
Garnish: sour cream, salsa

Layer sausage, chiles, pepper mixture and cheese in a greased slow cooker. Repeat layers until all ingredients except eggs and garnish are used, ending with a layer of cheese. Pour eggs over top. Cover and cook on low setting for 7 to 8 hours. Garnish as desired. Serves 10.

Invite sleepyheads out of bed...play a little mariachi music
while serving up South-of-the-Border Breakfast...olé!

Herbal Apple Tea

Regina Wickline
Pebble Beach, CA

A spiced tea the whole family can enjoy.

3 cinnamon herbal teabags
3 c. boiling water
2 c. apple juice

6 whole cloves
4-inch cinnamon stick

Place teabags in a slow cooker. Pour boiling water over top; let stand for 10 minutes. Remove and discard teabags. Add apple juice, cloves and cinnamon stick. Cover and cook on low setting for 2 to 3 hours. Remove and discard cloves and cinnamon stick. Makes 4 servings.

Warm up on a frosty morning with a big mug of herbal tea...
just for fun, stir it with a cherry licorice whip!

Viennese Coffee

Robin Hill
Rochester, NY

This traditional recipe is very rich tasting.

3 c. strong brewed coffee
3 T. chocolate syrup
1 t. sugar
1/3 c. whipping cream

Optional: 1/4 c. chocolate
   liqueur
Garnish: whipped topping,
   chocolate shavings or curls

Combine coffee, chocolate syrup and sugar in a slow cooker. Cover
and cook on low setting 2 to 2-1/2 hours. Stir in whipping cream
and liqueur, if using. Cover and cook on low setting for an additional
30 minutes, or until heated through. Ladle into mugs; garnish with
dollops of whipped topping and chocolate shavings, as desired.
Makes 4 servings.

Sweetest Day is October 20...leave a plump pumpkin, along
with a thermos of herbal tea, spiced cider or steamy
Viennese Coffee on the doorstep of someone special.

Breakie Potatoes

Laura Fuller
Fort Wayne, IN

Otherwise known as Breakfast Potatoes...our 3-year old always wants to know "What's for breakie?"

4 potatoes, peeled and sliced
1 T. butter, diced
1 onion, thinly sliced
4 slices bacon, crisply cooked
   and crumbled

1 c. shredded sharp Cheddar
   cheese

Layer half of each ingredient in slow cooker in this order: potatoes, butter, onion, bacon, cheese; repeat layering. Cover and cook on low setting for 8 to 10 hours. Makes 4 servings.

Rise & Shine Ham

Carrie O'Shea
Marina Del Rey, CA

The aroma of this breakfast ham will get even the toughest sleepyheads out of bed!

6 to 8-lb. picnic ham, trimmed
64-oz. bottle apple juice
1 c. brown sugar, packed

3 to 4 T. apple jelly
2 T. maple syrup

Trim skin and excess fat from ham. Place onto a cutting board. With a sharp knife, score ham in a diamond pattern, making cuts about one to 1-1/2 inches apart. Place ham into slow cooker flat-side down. Pour in enough apple juice to cover. Cover and cook on low setting for 6 hours. Transfer to a lightly greased baking sheet; set aside. Mix brown sugar, apple jelly and maple syrup together in a bowl; spread onto ham. Bake at 375 degrees for 30 to 40 minutes, or until topping is bubbling and glazed. Serves 8 to 10.

Eggs with Cheddar & Bacon

Lora Montgomery
Gooseberry Patch

*For a twist, try maple-flavored bacon or even pepper bacon
in this recipe.*

3 to 4 c. crusty bread, diced
1/2 lb. bacon, crisply cooked,
    crumbled and 1 T. drippings
    reserved
Optional: 2 to 3 c. favorite
    vegetables, chopped

8 eggs, beaten
1/2 c. milk
1 c. shredded Cheddar cheese
salt and pepper to taste

Place bread in a lightly greased slow cooker. If using vegetables,
heat reserved drippings in a large skillet over medium heat. Sauté
vegetables, tossing to coat. Stir bacon and vegetables into bread.
Whisk together eggs and milk in a medium bowl; stir in cheese,
salt and pepper. Pour over bread mixture. Cover and cook on low
setting for 3 to 3-1/2 hours, until eggs are set. Makes 6 to 8 servings.

Enjoy breakfast on the porch for a change. An old wooden
crate, once used to store fruit, is just the right size
for toting flatware and napkins to the table.

Sharon's Granola

Sharon Demers
Dolores, CO

This is a very easy and tasty recipe. Add any combination of raisins, dried fruit or nuts to suit your taste.

5 c. long-cooking oats,
   uncooked
1/2 c. oil
1/2 c. honey

1 t. vanilla extract
1 t. cinnamon
1 c. sweetened flaked coconut
1/8 t. salt

Mix all ingredients together and place in a slow cooker sprayed with non-stick vegetable spray. Cover, leaving lid slightly ajar. Cook on low setting for 5 hours, or until golden, stirring occasionally. Makes 6 servings.

Depending on the season,
wrap a bittersweet vine
or daisy chain around
an ice-filled sap bucket
or tin pail...a country-style
cooler for bottles of juice
or pint-size cartons of milk.

Early Bird Oatmeal

Lynda Robson
Boston, MA

You'll never have "plain" oatmeal again!

3 c. long-cooking oats,
   uncooked
3/4 c. powdered sugar
1/4 t. salt

21-oz. can cherry pie filling
6 c. water
1 t. almond extract

Combine oats, powdered sugar and salt in a large bowl; pour into a slow cooker that has been sprayed with non-stick vegetable spray. Add remaining ingredients; stir until combined. Cover and cook on low setting for 8 hours. Serves 4 to 6.

It's easy to find cookie jars in all shapes, sizes and colors.
Choose one with real personality...terrific for cookies,
of course, but it will also make a super flower vase.

Mamaw's Breakfast Cobbler

Melanie Lowe
Dover, DE

My grandma makes this breakfast treat whenever we visit her at the farm. It's always a wonderful time...gathering eggs, riding horses and staying up way past bedtime!

2 c. tart apples, cored, peeled and sliced	1 t. cinnamon
2 c. granola cereal	1/4 c. honey
	2 T. butter, melted

Combine apples, cereal and cinnamon in a lightly greased slow cooker and mix well. Stir together honey and butter; drizzle over apple mixture. Blend gently. Cover and cook on low setting for 8 hours, until apples are tender. Serves 4.

I had rather be on my farm than be emperor of the world.
-George Washington

Double-Delicious Cider

Tori Willis
Champaign, IL

Combine sweet apple juice with tangy orange juice, then add red cinnamon candies...this cider can't be beat!

4 c. apple juice
12-oz. can frozen orange juice
   concentrate, thawed
1/2 c. water
1 T. red cinnamon candies

1/2 t. ground nutmeg
1 t. whole cloves
Optional: orange slices,
   cinnamon sticks

Combine apple juice, orange juice concentrate, water, candies and nutmeg. Place cloves in a double thickness of cheesecloth; bring up corners of cloth and tie with kitchen string to form a bag. Add bag to slow cooker. Cover and cook on low setting for 2 to 3 hours. Before serving, discard spice bag and stir cider. Garnish with orange slices and cinnamon sticks, if desired. Makes 8 servings.

Pack a picnic on a winter's day! Take a hike in the woods, throw snowballs, build a snowman alongside a country road. When you're ready to warm up, your slow cooker will have a hearty meal waiting just for you.

Nutty Breakfast Cereal

Nola Coons
Gooseberry Patch

Pour a little warm milk over individual servings...yummy.

7 c. long-cooking oats,
   uncooked
1/2 c. powdered milk
Optional: 1 c. chopped walnuts

1/2 c. oil
1 c. creamy peanut butter
3/4 c. honey

Combine oats, powdered milk and walnuts, if using, in a slow cooker. Add remaining ingredients without mixing. Cook, uncovered, on high setting for one hour. Stir when honey and peanut butter are slightly melted. Reduce to low setting and continue to cook, uncovered, for an additional 2 to 3 hours. Serves 6 to 8.

Mom's Rice Porridge

Samantha Sparks
Madison, WI

You can use either medium-grain or short-grain rice in this recipe.

1 c. long-cooking rice, uncooked
2 c. water
1-1/2 c. evaporated milk

1/2 t. salt
1/2 c. raisins

Combine all the ingredients in a slow cooker. Cover and cook on low setting for 6 to 8 hours, or overnight. Serves 2 to 4.

Desserts

Mom's Blueberry Cobbler

Sharon Tillman
Hampton, VA

Growing up, I always loved blueberries...I still do! Mom would make this easy recipe which uses pie filling so I could have her yummy cobbler any time of year.

2 8-oz. tubes refrigerated
   biscuits, separated and
   quartered
1/3 c. brown sugar, packed

1/2 t. cinnamon
1/3 c. butter, melted
21-oz. can blueberry pie filling

Spray a slow cooker with non-stick vegetable spray and layer one package of biscuits inside. In a small bowl, mix together brown sugar, cinnamon and melted butter just until combined; sprinkle half the mixture over biscuit layer. Spread half the pie filling over top. Layer remaining biscuits; sprinkle with remaining brown sugar mixture and top with remaining pie filling. Cover and cook on high setting for 2-1/2 to 3 hours, until biscuits are golden. Makes 6 to 8 servings.

Tote a slow cooker (or several) to a potluck in the park.
A quick-fix canopy is easy to create with fabric and tall
garden stakes. Insert the stakes into the ground, then
drape fabric over the stakes and your car or truck luggage
rack...secure with ribbon. So simple!

Tropical Cobbler

*Cheri Maxwell
Gulf Breeze, FL*

Pineapple brings a refreshing flavor to homestyle cobbler.

18-1/2 oz. pkg. yellow cake mix   Garnish: whipped topping
20-oz. can crushed pineapple

Set aside 1/3 cup dry cake mix. Spray a slow cooker with non-stick vegetable spray; sprinkle half of remaining dry cake mix in slow cooker. Spread half the crushed pineapple with juice over cake mix. Repeat layering. Sprinkle reserved cake mix over final layer of pineapple. Cover and cook on high setting for 2 hours. Serve with whipped topping. Makes 6 to 8 servings.

Hillside Orchard Compote

*Rhonda Reeder
Ellicott City, MD*

While we love trips to our local orchard, this compote recipe is the one I turn to when I want to toss it together and forget about it.

2 29-oz. cans sliced peaches,
    drained
2 29-oz. can pear halves,
    drained and sliced
20-oz. can pineapple chunks,
    drained

15-1/4 oz. apricot halves,
    drained and sliced
21-oz. can cherry pie filling

In a slow cooker, combine peaches, pears, pineapple and apricots. Top with pie filling. Cover and cook on high setting for 2 hours, or until heated through. Serve with a slotted spoon. Makes 14 to 18 servings.

Southern Caramel Pie

Judy Collins
Nashville, TN

Here in Nashville, one of the country clubs always served the most delicious caramel pie made with sweetened condensed milk. This recipe is an easy way to make that wonderful tasting caramel pie in the slow cooker.

2 14-oz. cans sweetened condensed milk	Garnish: whipped topping
9-inch graham cracker crust	Optional: mini semi-sweet chocolate chips

Pour condensed milk into a slow cooker that has been sprayed with non-stick vegetable spray. Cover and cook on low setting for 3-1/2 to 4 hours, stirring every 15 minutes after 2-1/2 hours. Spoon into crust (the mixture should be golden and should be spooned in before it gets too thick). Chill well. Top with whipped topping and chocolate chips if desired. Cooking time could vary depending on size of your slow cooker. Mixture will appear lumpy, but will thin with stirring. Makes 6 to 8 servings.

It's easy to transform any flat smooth surface into a handy kitchen blackboard... try a dustpan or enamel bakeware! Apply 2 coats of chalkboard paint, taping off any areas where you don't want paint; let dry. What a super spot to jot down grocery needs for favorite slow-cooker recipes!

Slow-Cooker Tapioca

Betty Kozlowski
Newnan, GA

My husband is very fond of tapioca, so I was delighted to find this recipe for the slow cooker.

2 qts. milk
1 c. pearled tapioca, uncooked
1 to 1-1/2 c. sugar

4 eggs, beaten
1 t. vanilla extract
Garnish: whipped cream, fruit

Combine milk, tapioca and sugar in a slow cooker; stir to mix. Cover and cook on high setting for 3 hours. In a large bowl, whisk together eggs and vanilla; gradually add hot milk mixture. Pour back into slow cooker. Cover and cook on high setting for an additional 20 minutes. Chill until ready to serve; garnish as desired. Serves 10 to 12.

Jot down all your favorite, tried & true slow-cooker recipes for a new bride who's just learning to cook. Tucked inside a brand new slow cooker, she'll love 'em both!

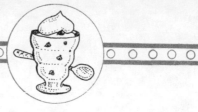

Apple-Cranberry Dessert

Megan Brooks
Antioch, TN

*Our family went to a country fair this past weekend and this was
being served at one of the vendor tents. They were kind enough
to share the recipe so now we can enjoy it at home too.*

6 apples, cored, peeled and
   sliced
1 c. cranberries
1 c. sugar

1/2 t. grated orange zest
1/2 c. water
3 T. port wine or orange juice
Optional: whipping cream

Arrange apples and cranberries in lightly greased slow cooker;
sprinkle with sugar. Add orange zest, water and wine or juice. Stir
to mix. Cover and cook on low setting for 4 to 6 hours, until apples
are tender. Spoon into serving bowls; pour cream over top, if desired.
Serves 6.

Some people like to paint pictures, or do gardening,
or build a boat in the basement. Other people get a tremendous
pleasure out of the kitchen, because cooking is just as creative
and imaginative an activity as drawing, or wood carving or music.

-Julia Child

Country-Style Bread Pudding

Patricia Wissler
Harrisburg, PA

This is the best tasting bread pudding ever, and so much easier than making it in the oven.

3/4 c. brown sugar, packed
6 slices cinnamon-raisin bread,
  buttered and cubed
4 eggs, beaten

1 qt. milk
1-1/2 t. vanilla extract

Sprinkle brown sugar in a slow cooker that has been sprayed with non-stick vegetable spray. Add cubed bread without stirring. In a large bowl, beat together eggs, milk and vanilla; pour over bread. Cover and cook on high setting for 2 to 3 hours, until thickened. Do not stir. Spoon pudding into individual serving dishes and drizzle brown sugar sauce from slow cooker over pudding. Makes 8 to 10 servings.

If it's time to buy a new slow cooker, look for one with a removable crock...they're so much easier to clean!

A Bunch of Crunch Candy

Marlene Darnell
Newport Beach, CA

My son took this candy to school to share with friends...
it was an instant hit!

2 lbs. white melting chocolate,
   broken into small pieces
1-1/2 c. creamy peanut butter
Optional: 1/2 t. almond extract

4 c. corn & oat cereal
4 c. crispy rice cereal
4 c. mini marshmallows

Place chocolate in a slow cooker. Cover and cook on high setting for one hour. Add peanut butter; stir in extract, if desired. In a large bowl, combine cereals and marshmallows. Stir into chocolate mixture until well coated. Drop by tablespoonfuls onto wax paper; let stand until set. Store at room temperature. Makes about 6-1/2 dozen.

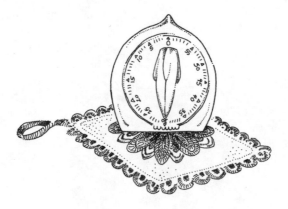

Don't worry about slow-cooking temperatures being below what's considered safe for cooking. The Low setting is about 200 degrees, while the High setting is about 300 degrees...both well above the safe temperature of 140 degrees.

Nutty Chocolate Clusters

Amy Crowe-Galloway
Pontotoc, MS

Try peanut butter chips in this recipe instead of the semi-sweet chocolate chips...simply wonderful!

2 lbs. white melting chocolate, chopped
4-oz. pkg. sweet baking chocolate, chopped

12-oz. pkg. semi-sweet chocolate chips
24-oz. jar dry roasted peanuts

Mix together all ingredients; add to a slow cooker. Cover and cook for one hour on high setting. Do not stir. Reduce to low setting. Cover and cook for one hour, stirring every 15 minutes. Drop onto wax paper and let cool. Store in an airtight container. Makes about 4-1/2 pounds.

Slow cookers are super year 'round...no matter what the occasion. So grab a friend and head out to the local craft show, barn sale, swap meet or small-town county fair. When you come home, a delicious meal or dessert will be waiting for you!

Carol's Strawberry Fondue

Nancy Wise
Little Rock, AR

My friend, Carol, has a farm outside of town. Along with a menagerie of animals and a huge garden, she has an amazing strawberry patch. One summer we spent an afternoon just slicing berries to freeze...while they were scrumptious in this recipe, frozen berries from the grocer work just as well.

10-oz. pkg. frozen sliced
   strawberries, thawed
1/4 c. half-and-half
1 t. cornstarch

1/2 t. lemon juice
angel food cake cubes, fresh
   fruit

Combine strawberries, half-and-half, cornstarch and lemon juice in a food processor or blender; process until smooth. Pour into saucepan. Bring to a boil over medium heat; cook and stir for 2 minutes, or until slightly thickened. Transfer to a slow cooker on low setting to keep warm. Serve with cake cubes and fruit. Makes 1-1/2 cups.

Visit a farmers' market or roadside stand for the freshest berries to dip in fondue.

Razzleberry Upside-Down Cake

Donna Fisher
Gooseberry Patch

The name makes us giggle, but this cake is so delicious we make one almost every week. The kids love to just spoon this out of the slow cooker.

3 egg whites
1-1/4 c. water
1/3 c. applesauce
.3-oz. pkg. sugar-free raspberry
 gelatin mix

18-1/4 oz. pkg. cherry chip
 cake mix
12-oz. can red raspberry pastry
 filling

With an electric mixer on high speed, beat egg whites for one to 2 minutes, until soft peaks form. Add water, applesauce, gelatin mix and cake mix; beat on medium speed for 2 minutes. Spread raspberry filling into a slow cooker that has been sprayed with non-stick vegetable spray; pour cake batter mixture over top. Do not stir. Cover with 8 paper towels. Cover and cook on high setting for 2 hours. Remove crock from slow cooker; let cool for 15 minutes. Place a large rimmed serving plate on top of slow cooker. Carefully invert cake onto plate. Serves 10 to 12.

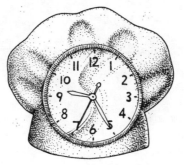

If you need to alter slow-cooker settings, keep this rule in mind...one hour on High is equal to 2 hours on Low.

Chocolate-Peanut Butter Cake

Rogene Rogers
Bemidji, MN

This cake is made in a coffee can. When it's done, I take it out of the coffee can, slice and drizzle servings with a little hot fudge sauce. This is a sure-fire cure for chocolate and peanut butter cravings!

18-1/2 oz. pkg. chocolate
  cake mix, divided
1/2 c. water

1/3 c. creamy peanut butter
1/2 c. chopped nuts

Measure 2 cups cake mix into a large bowl; reserve remaining mix for another recipe. Add remaining ingredients to bowl; mix well. Beat by hand for about 2 minutes. Pour into a greased and floured 2-pound metal coffee can. Place can in slow cooker; cover top of can with 8 paper towels to absorb condensation. Cover and cook on high setting for 2 to 3 hours. Cool for 5 minutes. Slice a knife around edge of can and carefully turn out cake. Makes 10 to 12 servings.

Need to measure a sticky ingredient like peanut butter?
A quick spritz of non-stick cooking spray inside
the measuring cup and it'll slide out easily.

Hot Fudge Brownies

Jewel Sharpe
Raleigh, NC

*This is a favorite recipe I make for camping trips...
a chocolatey dessert everyone loves.*

20-oz. pkg. brownie mix
1 c. chocolate syrup
1 c. hot water

Optional: vanilla ice cream,
whipped topping

Prepare brownies according to package instructions. Spray a slow cooker with non-stick vegetable spray. Spread brownie batter evenly into slow cooker. Mix together syrup and hot water; pour evenly over brownie mixture. Cook on high setting for 2-1/2 to 3 hours, until edges are set. Remove lid; let stand for 30 minutes, until set. Spoon onto serving plates. Serve with ice cream or whipped topping, if desired. Serves 8.

Watch for vintage syrup pitchers at flea markets...fill 'em up
with caramel, strawberry, double fudge or butterscotch
ice cream toppings and serve with Hot Fudge Brownies.

Banana Pudding Cake

Vickie

*My grandson loves to drizzle chocolate syrup on servings, then top
with whipped cream and a cherry...his version of a banana split!*

3 egg whites
1 c. bananas, mashed
2-1/2 c. water, divided

18-1/2 oz. pkg. yellow cake mix
3-oz. pkg. cook & serve banana
   pudding mix

With an electric mixer on high speed, beat egg whites until soft peaks
form, about one to 2 minutes. In a separate bowl, beat bananas until
puréed; add to egg whites. Mix together 1/2 cup water, banana mixture
and dry cake mix and beat for one to 2 minutes; set aside. Spray
slow cooker with non-stick vegetable spray. In a small bowl, combine
remaining water and dry pudding mix, stirring until dissolved. Pour
cake mixture and pudding mixture into slow cooker; do not stir. Place
a paper towel on top to absorb moisture. Cover and cook on high
setting for 2 hours. Place a large rimmed serving plate on top of slow
cooker. Carefully invert cake onto plate. Serves 12.

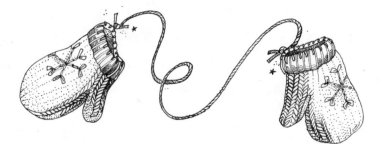

As winter approaches, host a dessert get-together with
friends and ask each to bring a gently-worn winter coat
or pair of new mittens. Donate them to a local shelter...
kindness that will warm the chilly days ahead.

Peachy Dump Cake

Autry Dotson
Sedalia, MO

*Equally scrumptious with cherry or apple pie filling...
try any favorite flavor, you can't miss!*

2 14-1/2 oz. cans peach
  pie filling
1 t. lemon juice
18-1/2 oz. pkg. yellow cake mix

1/2 c. chopped pecans
1/2 c. butter, melted
Garnish: whipped topping,
  vanilla ice cream

Pour pie filling into a slow cooker that has been sprayed with
non-stick vegetable spray. Drizzle with lemon juice. In a separate
bowl, combine dry cake mix, pecans and melted butter. Spread over
pie filling. Cover and cook on low setting for 4 hours, or on high
setting for 2 hours. Serve with whipped cream or ice cream. Makes
6 to 8 servings.

Dress up a dessert buffet table...tiered cake plates are
so pretty for displaying votives.

Honeyed Apple Treat

Connie Bryant
Topeka, KS

This dessert is one my friend Ellen shared with our family when I was feeling a bit under the weather. She brought along a dozen fresh eggs from her hens as well...what a farmgirl!

4 tart apples, cored, peeled and sliced
2 c. granola with fruit and nuts
1/4 c. honey

2 T. butter, melted
1 t. cinnamon
Garnish: whipped topping
Optional: nutmeg

Combine apples and cereal in a slow cooker. In a separate bowl, combine honey, butter, cinnamon and nutmeg, if using; pour over apple mixture and mix well. Cover and cook on low setting for 6 to 8 hours. Garnish with whipped topping; sprinkle with nutmeg, if desired. Serves 4 to 6.

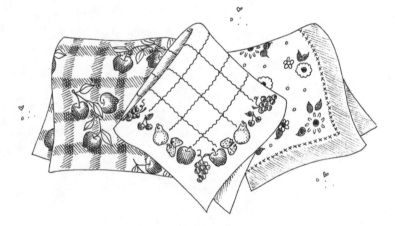

Colorful vintage-style oilcloth makes the best-ever tablecloth, or trim it to placemat size...it wipes clean in a jiffy!

Slow-Cooked Brown Sugar Apples
Lynn Williams
Muncie, IN

*Nothing says comfort like the aroma of these apples cooking...
unless, of course, it's sitting down to enjoy them.*

6 apples, cored
3/4 c. orange juice
1/2 c. apple cider

1/4 t. cinnamon
1/2 c. brown sugar, packed
Optional: whipped topping

Peel a strip around the top of each apple to help prevent cracking.
Arrange apples in a slow cooker. In large bowl, combine remaining
ingredients except whipped topping; mix to blend. Spoon over apples.
Cover and cook on low setting for 3 to 4 hours, until apples are
tender. Cool slightly and serve warm with whipped topping, if desired.
Makes 6 servings.

Fill old-fashioned glass
salt shakers with powdered
sugar, cinnamon or nutmeg.
They make the prettiest
little containers for dusting
dessert servings with
a bit of sweetness.

Upside-Down Blueberry Cake

Missie Brown
Gooseberry Patch

Keep it simple...just spoon this cake out if you don't want to invert the slow cooker.

21-oz. can blueberry pie filling
2 eggs
18-1/4 oz. pkg. lemon cake mix

1 c. water
1/3 c. applesauce

Spread pie filling in a slow cooker that has been sprayed with non-stick vegetable spray. With an electric mixer on high speed, beat egg whites until soft peaks form, about 2 minutes. Stir in remaining ingredients just until combined. Pour over filling; do not stir. Place 8 paper towels on top of slow cooker to absorb moisture. Cover and cook on high setting for 2 hours, or until a toothpick tests clean when inserted near center. Remove crock from slow cooker; remove lid and paper towel. Cool cake for 15 minutes. Place a large serving plate over crock; carefully invert onto plate. Serves 10 to 12.

Take dessert outdoors...spread a quilt or fleece blanket on a picnic table or under a shady tree and enjoy the sunshine!

Berry Patch Shortcake

Cathy Hillier
Salt Lake City, UT

We have a pick-your-own berry patch just down the road from our home...one Saturday we took the kids and had a grand time!

2-1/4 c. pancake mix
3/4 c. sugar, divided
2/3 c. milk
3 T. applesauce

1 qt. strawberries, hulled
 and sliced
Garnish: whipped topping

Combine pancake mix, 1/2 cup sugar, milk and applesauce; stir until a dough forms. Spray a slow cooker with non-stick vegetable spray. Pat dough into bottom of slow cooker. Cover and cook on high setting for one hour and 15 minutes, or until toothpick tests clean when inserted into center. Toss together strawberries and remaining sugar. Turn shortcake out of slow cooker; slice into wedges and split. Spoon berries over top; dollop with whipped topping. Serves 8.

Try these easy (and memorable) dessert topping ideas... gummy fruit candy, fluffy whipped topping, conversation hearts, mini chocolate chips, sprinkles or a drizzle of chocolate syrup. Sweet and simple.

Super-Simple Caramel Rolls

Geneva Rogers
Gillette, WY

*I love to make caramel rolls from scratch...but when time's short,
this slow-cooker version means I can head out the door to my
favorite barn sale or auction!*

1/2 c. brown sugar, packed   1/4 c. butter, melted
1/2 t. cinnamon
2 8-oz. tubes refrigerated
   biscuits, separated

Mix together brown sugar and cinnamon. Dip biscuits into melted
butter, then into brown sugar mixture; place into a greased slow
cooker. Cover and cook on high setting for 2-1/2 to 3 hours, until
rolls are cooked through. Makes 6 to 8 servings.

Touchdown Butterscotch Dip

Melanie Lowe
Dover, DE

Mom likes to make this when the "big game" is on!

2 11-oz. pkgs. butterscotch   2/3 c. chopped pecans
   chips   1 T. rum extract
5-oz. can evaporated milk   apple and pear wedges

Combine butterscotch chips and evaporated milk in a slow cooker.
Cover and cook on low setting for 45 to 50 minutes, or until chips
are softened; stir until smooth. Stir in pecans and extract. Serve warm
with fruit. Makes about 3 cups.

Falltime Snackin' Cake

Annette Ingram
Grand Rapids, MI

This is one recipe I make and take along when we're on the road for autumn leaf peeping...paired with a thermos of cider, we're all set!

18-1/2 oz. pkg. yellow cake mix   3/4 c. maple syrup
4 eggs, beaten   2 T. applesauce

Combine all ingredients; pour into slow cooker that has been sprayed with non-stick vegetable spray. Place a paper towel over slow cooker to absorb moisture. Cover and cook on high setting for 2 hours. Uncover; invert a serving plate over top and turn out cake. Cool for 10 minutes. Makes 10 to 12 servings.

To save clean-up time, use cold water, not hot to
wash bowls eggs were beaten in...surprisingly, hot water
makes the egg tougher to remove!

Cherry-Chocolate Dessert

Sue Learned
Wilton, CA

This is almost like eating a sweet chocolate-covered cherry...yummy!

21-oz. can cherry pie filling
18-1/2 oz. pkg. chocolate
   cake mix

1/2 c. butter, melted

Pour pie filling into a slow cooker and set aside. Combine dry cake mix and melted butter; sprinkle over filling. Cover and cook on low setting for 3 hours. Spoon into serving dishes. Serves 10 to 12.

Chocolate Concoction

Marcia Masters
The Woodlands, TX

Sooo good...there's nothing else I can say!

18-1/4 oz. pkg. devil's food
   cake mix
16-oz. container sour cream
3.9-oz. pkg. instant chocolate
   pudding mix
1-1/2 c. semi-sweet chocolate
   chips

4 eggs, beaten
1 c. water
Optional: French vanilla
   ice cream

Beat together all ingredients except ice cream until smooth. Pour into a slow cooker that has been sprayed with non-stick vegetable spray. Cover and cook on low setting for 6 to 8 hours. Serve with ice cream, if desired. Makes 8 to 10 servings.

Rogene's Homestyle Custard

Rogene Rogers
Bemidji, MN

We love old-fashioned baked custard and enjoy this version made in the slow cooker. If you like, add 1/4 cup sweetened flaked coconut.

2 c. milk
5 eggs, beaten
1/3 c. super-fine sugar

1 t. vanilla extract
1/8 t. salt
1/4 t. nutmeg

Mix together all ingredients except nutmeg in a large bowl; pour into a slow cooker. Sprinkle nutmeg over top. Cover and cook on low setting for 8 hours. Serves 4 to 6.

Pull out those fanciful, flowery teacups tucked away for "someday." They're just the right size for holding sweet servings of custards, bread puddings and cobblers.

INDEX

INDEX

Sandwiches

INDEX

Send us your favorite recipe!

and the memory that makes it special for you! If we select your recipe for a brand-new **Gooseberry Patch** cookbook, your name will appear right along with it...and you'll receive a FREE copy of the book.

Share your recipe on our website at
www.gooseberrypatch.com

Or mail to:

Gooseberry Patch • Attn: Cookbook Dept.
2500 Farmers Dr., #110 • Columbus, OH 43235

*Don't forget to include your name, address, phone number and email address so we'll know how to reach you for your FREE book!

Since 1992, we've been publishing country cookbooks for every kitchen and for every meal of the day! Each has hundreds of budget-friendly recipes, using ingredients you already have on hand. Their lay-flat binding makes them easy to use and each is filled with hand-drawn artwork and plenty of personality.

Have a taste for more?

Call us toll-free at
1•800•854•6673

Find us here too!

Join our **Circle of Friends** and discover free recipes & crafts, plus giveaways & more!

Visit our website or blog to join and be sure to follow us on Facebook & Twitter too.

www.gooseberrypatch.com

Join Our Circle of Friends

Find Gooseberry Patch in Your Neighborhood

Find us on Facebook

You Tube

Follow us on **twitter**

Read Our Blog

U.S. to Canadian recipe equivalents

Volume Measurements

1/4 teaspoon	1 mL
1/2 teaspoon	2 mL
1 teaspoon	5 mL
1 tablespoon = 3 teaspoons	15 mL
2 tablespoons = 1 fluid ounce	30 mL
1/4 cup	60 mL
1/3 cup	75 mL
1/2 cup = 4 fluid ounces	125 mL
1 cup = 8 fluid ounces	250 mL
2 cups = 1 pint =16 fluid ounces	500 mL
4 cups = 1 quart	1 L

Weights

1 ounce	30 g
4 ounces	120 g
8 ounces	225 g
16 ounces = 1 pound	450 g

Oven Temperatures

300° F	150° C
325° F	160° C
350° F	180° C
375° F	190° C
400° F	200° C
450° F	230° C

Baking Pan Sizes

Square	
8x8x2 inches	2 L = 20x20x5 cm
9x9x2 inches	2.5 L = 23x23x5 cm

Rectangular	
13x9x2 inches	3.5 L = 33x23x5 cm

Loaf	
9x5x3 inches	2 L = 23x13x7 cm

Round	
8x1-1/2 inches	1.2 L = 20x4 cm
9x1-1/2 inches	1.5 L = 23x4 cm